COMING UP
FOR AIR

Also by Tom Daley:

My Story
Tom's Daily Plan
Tom's Daily Goals

TOM DALEY

COMING UP FOR AIR

ONE PLACE. MANY STORIES

HQ
An imprint of HarperCollins*Publishers* Ltd
1 London Bridge Street
London SE1 9GF

www.harpercollins.co.uk

HarperCollins*Publishers*
1st Floor, Watermarque Building, Ringsend Road
Dublin 4, Ireland

This edition 2021

1
First published in Great Britain by
HQ, an imprint of HarperCollins*Publishers* Ltd 2021

HB ISBN: 978-0-00-821791-4
TPB ISBN: 978-0-00-848773-7

MIX
Paper from
responsible sources

FSC
www.fsc.org FSC™ C007454

This book is produced from independently certified FSC™ paper
to ensure responsible forest management.

For more information visit: www.harpercollins.co.uk/green

Typeset in Sabon by Palimpsest Book Production Ltd, Falkirk, Stirlingshire

Printed and Bound in the UK using 100% Renewable Electricity
at CPI Group (UK) Ltd

For Robbie and Lance, whose love made
me fly higher than I ever thought possible.

CONTENTS

INTRODUCTION

As I walked to the end of the ten-metre board, I glanced down. The distinctive pattern of the interlocking rings and the words 'London 2012' shone through the bright blue of the water. Olympic banners were plastered across every available wall, along with flags of the participating countries, and my own face grinned back at me on various enormous screens sitting high above the stands. The atmosphere was electric; it was a cacophony of noise from the PA system, as well as cheers, shouts and applause from the crowd. The sound ricocheted around the domed, undulating ceilings of the London Aquatics Centre. It was almost deafening.

I inhaled slowly and steadily. The air was thick with the sticky warmth of chlorine and the charged crowd. I needed to focus hard. My heart pounded to the tips of my fingers.

It takes 1.6 seconds between leaving the board and hitting the water. The importance of the approaching 1.6 seconds was not lost on me.

This was it: the Olympic final and the moment I had dreamed of, and worked for, my whole life.

The whistle blew and an eerie silence settled. All I could hear was the gentle and rhythmic gurgle and swoosh of water as it flowed in the drains.

I adored the buzz of the home crowd. There were 18,000 people at the pool and the main BBC channels had tuned in to the diving. I knew I carried the hopes of many on my shoulders and that millions of pairs of eyes would be on me from sofas, kitchens and gardens, along with the focus of the seven judges who would mark the execution of my dives, but the pressure felt like a positive thing. It felt like an almighty fizz and rush of adrenalin. For most athletes, competing at an Olympic Games is a once-in-a-lifetime opportunity. To compete in front of a home crowd at an Olympic Games is something very few people ever get to experience. I knew I was very fortunate. I needed to just enjoy myself and, in the words of my dad, 'Dive my socks off'.

I was about to launch into my first dive of six – the Twister. This dive consists of a sequence of moves as my body snaps into different positions in the air like elastic: I jump into the air, then move into a twisting position to complete two and a half twists; at the same time I am somersaulting two and a half times. I finish the last somersault in a pike position – knees straight and body bent at the waist – before ripping into the water, like a bullet.

Before the Olympic Games, this was my 'safest' dive and one I knew I could perform well. It was one of my harder dives but executed correctly, the rewards were high. In each individual diving competition, there are six dives: a forward dive, facing forwards when we take off; a backward dive, taking off with our backs to the water; reverse dives where we face the water, take off forwards and rotate backwards towards the board; an inward dive, where we face the back of the board, jump backwards and rotate forwards towards the board; a handstand dive; and a twisting dive. The Twister is the twisting dive that every elite diver performs. This was the one dive that I always knew I could confidently score over 90 points. The Twister always opened my set and was the one dive that I used to kick off each competition because I knew it could propel me towards the top of the leader board.

A good place to be.

But in the run-up to the Games, small things had started to go wrong. There were times that I had leant a little bit too far back and landed awkwardly on my side or shoulder, or when I got lost in the dive and would be flailing through the air without knowing which way was up and which way was down. One day, I landed gracelessly on my back with an almighty smack and on another, I wrenched my neck. My confidence had been slowly chipped away. The possibilities of what could go wrong lurked like shadows in the back of my mind.

I had made it through the prelims and the semis of the individual event, and the numbers had been whittled down from thirty-two divers to eighteen and then to twelve. The reigning Olympic champion, Matthew Mitcham, had finished in an agonising thirteenth place in the semis. It can happen – one bad dive of six and you were out – but I was still in the game. My prelim was one of my worst performances in competitions for a long time and I had finished fifteenth out of eighteen places. As the pressure mounted there had been an uplift in the numbers across the board, as each of the competitors bettered our last performance and the scores crept up. But regardless of the numbers, those earlier competitions were over with, and at that moment they were no longer important. It was always just about making it to the finals. Each dive was a completely independent event. I knew at the end of those six dives, I would either be an Olympic medallist or not.

I took off, rolling into a twist, twisting two and a half times with one arm across my body and the other to my head, before rolling into a sharp and precise pike position to somersault two and a half times forwards. In my dives, I have to be hyper-vigilant and 'spot' the water – I need to see everything in order to count the rotations, so I know where my body is in the air. I'm not just spinning in one direction; there are a lot of movements going on at once and I need to keep every part of my body in the right place at the right millisecond, like an innate internal compass. There is not an opportunity to think about anything else but precisely what I am doing in that instant. At that moment, my focus has to be razor-sharp; there is no space to blink or even breathe. The world whizzes by in a somewhat organised blur. I often see other things as I rotate or twist – faces, flashes of wall, posters – but I can always spot the water, and I need to; it is the one constant in every diving pool.

As I spun and tried to spot the pool, I was blinded by a sudden and disarming white flash of cameras. The flashes sliced across my vision. I blinked, and there is no time to blink in that 1.6 seconds. I was confused and my brain felt dislocated from my body. I landed slightly short, not really knowing what had happened. As I entered the water I was not vertical; it felt a bit messy and I knew that it wasn't great.

As I climbed out of the water, I gestured to my coach, Andy Banks, and he could see what had happened. I felt a wave of anger and injustice roll over me. I had worked so hard for that moment and someone had inadvertently ruined my chances. The spectators at any diving competition are always told not to use flash photography. On that day, maybe they didn't realise the importance of this instruction, perhaps they did not realise their flashes were clicked on, or possibly some people's cameras had gone off automatically. It was impossible to know why. The scores came up on the board – it was unanimous '7s' and an overall score of 75.60 – certainly not enough to give me a chance at one of the top medals.

Andy walked over to the referee and, after a few moments, called me over too. I had never in my entire diving career, up until that point, or since, had to do this. I was terrified. I almost didn't know what had happened – like the moment had been wiped from my brain – and I struggled to relay it to him.

I felt almost winded.

The referee looked at me.

'I get that there's a home crowd advantage and I've got people cheering for me, but this is like a home crowd dis-advantage,' I said breathlessly, trying to convey my point, without getting too emotional. 'They're clearly not turning camera flashes off. I was massively distracted all the way through that dive. And can you please tell them to turn it off to not ruin it for any other divers?'

'What are you asking?' He raised his tanned eyebrows.

'Please can we have a re-dive?' Andy chipped in.

For a moment I felt guilty; everyone – the crowd, the other divers on the poolside, their teams – was waiting for me, and was I making too much of a fuss about it? Maybe I should just accept it as bad luck? One of those things that was outside of my control? I doubted myself.

The assistant referee came over and they conferred together before the older one gestured to the tower. He told me to re-take the dive.

My eyes felt like they had popped out of my skull with the shock. I had never thought that he would agree.

When you get lost in a dive, there is a process to rebreak and rebuild the whole movement; you usually start from scratch and it can take months. I had seconds.

The pressure at that moment felt monumental but I knew I had to do it. I had worked as hard as anyone else to get to that point. I took a swig of water and made my way up the stairs to the ten-metre board as fast as I could, trying to go through the familiar process of rehearsing and visualising the dive in my head a couple of times before I reached the top.

A voice came over the PA system.

'Ladies and gentlemen, please listen very carefully. Tom Daley has been awarded a re-dive by FINA. He has been awarded the re-dive because he was distracted during his dive due to the use of flash photography. You were asked at the beginning to ensure that there was no flash photography. Please could everybody ensure that flashes are turned off, or do not use your camera. Thank you very much.'

The pressure to do well just minutes beforehand now felt suffocating. If I was anxious before, the feelings of adrenalin had switched from excitement into an almost overwhelming panic. There was a sea of people, eyes piercing mine. Some people just waved and cheered from the stands; they were clearly not really sure what had happened and were just excited to see another dive. Nearer, on the poolside, I could see some of the diving team, their heads clutched tightly in their laps with their whitened fists grasped over their ears because they didn't dare to watch me and what might happen next.

Every sense felt acutely magnified. My heart hammered like a drum into my head and my breath felt short. I tried to focus on the process of rehearsing the dive in my head and making my body was ready. I trembled as I wiped the sweat and moisture from my body with my shammy, so I didn't slip out of the dive. I felt the weight and load of my body on the balls of my feet and my toes on the edge of the platform more than I had ever done before. My vision felt suddenly sharp and narrow; it was almost kaleidoscopic. It felt like I was in a goldfish bowl and everyone was tapping angrily on the glass. I had to hold my focus and do the best that I could, however strangled I felt. I knew I couldn't rush and make another mistake that would be solely mine. I couldn't think about anything else.

All that mattered in that moment was the dive. I had to own it or I would crumble. I took a deep breath, counted myself in, and leaped into the air.

*　　*　　*

Despite standing on the podium hours after that dive, with the comforting weight of an Olympic medal around my neck and feeling the most incredible rush of elation, the subsequent weeks and months were some of the hardest that I have ever experienced. That incredible moment foreshadowed some complex, yet transformative years ahead. I was 18 and on the cusp of adulthood, complete freedom and independence.

The high of winning a medal was incredible, but it was also surprisingly short-lived. After the exhileration of my London 2012 experience came the rush of the Olympic blues: the lowest of lows that seemed to stick for far longer than the transitory triumph of my medal achievement. That moment of my re-dive manifested itself in a seismic sense of shock that made diving feel impossible at times. I was unsure of my future path and where it would lead me, and for a long time I blindly stumbled along, hoping that I could do something, anything, away from the pool because I was so scared. My previously honed focus started to slip away like sand through my fingers.

In the time since 2012, I've tackled many other hurdles, both on and off the diving board. I have suffered painful and protracted injuries where I wondered if I could continue pushing my body to dive through the constant slaps, bangs and pain. I've suffered concussions, a broken hand, and illnesses that have set me back physically and mentally. In

Rio, four years after London 2012, an Olympic Games where I was at my peak and there was an expectation that I would win gold, I crashed out of the individual semi-final event, experiencing a very public failure. With the support of my family and friends, I scraped myself back up and I came back a year later, stronger and fitter at the World Championships to beat the world's best.

During a chance meeting in LA in 2013, I met my soulmate and I fell head over heels in love and decided to come out, on my own terms, online. I got married and we now have a beautiful son; we are a family and my perspective has shifted and recalibrated dramatically. All this has happened under the watchful and opinionated gaze of the public, the media and my sport, and that has not been without its own challenges to navigate.

In this book, I hope to reflect on some important and significant moments over the last decade, and before, that have helped to shape me and guide me towards career and personal contentment and success. I have developed traits that have helped me reach my goals, and have learned many hard-won lessons. Here, I hope to share some of these with you.

PERSEVERANCE

When I look back on that winning moment in 2012, like a film reel on rewind and fast forward, it is only now that I can see with clarity how it impacted my life moving forwards. The effects of what had happened in that moment of my re-dive at the Olympic Games more than just dented my confidence: it caused a sense of shock that manifested itself in many other ways. The immediate euphoria of winning the bronze medal was phenomenal. I don't really remember much about that final at all – it is all a bit of a blur; there is nothing that sticks in my mind firmly except my re-dive and the incredible high that I felt when my hands ripped through the water on the last dive of my list and I knew I had won a medal. I felt like I could've leaped out of the water like a dolphin. But after that, I really struggled and had to channel deep to find inner reserves and resolve that I never knew I really had. All I had ever thought about was performing well at London 2012, and never about what would come after that. I hadn't even considered what it would feel like being a medal winner and then going on to the same circuit of relentless international competitions that I had always done – it hadn't occurred to me how much extra pressure being an Olympic medallist would bring with it. It was a struggle but I kept going, continued training and diving and, in doing so, it was a time of personal and professional growth. The path to success is never linear. But when you stick with it and persevere through the hard times you can make the most difference and provide a catalyst for change. I have seen that many times throughout my career, in the days and weeks when training feels unrelenting, but none more so than after 2012.

I had just turned 18 in the May before the Olympics, and after training so hard, I finally had a chance to go out and party and enjoy myself. After so many years of doing schoolwork and training and going from school to the pool and back again and almost nowhere else, I was able to experience a slice of normality with more parties and more fun. But I still trained hard and was back at the familiar pool in Plymouth a week after the Olympics to work towards the Junior World Championships in October.

My twisting dive was starting to become a huge mental block, and those worries that had been skulking in the back of my mind were now firmly at the forefront of everything. At the crux of it was the terror that the dive would go wrong. Hitting the water at a bad angle at thirty-five miles per hour is no joke. The right way to dive is a seamless combination of grace, power and precision. Twisting dives require rotating on two different axes: first your body twists, like a pirouette, before spinning into a somersault and rotating on that axis. There are different ways you can control the dive by changing your body shape – straightening the body in a somersault to slow the rotation or making yourself smaller to speed the rotation up. The process of practising the movements over and over again on dry land and in the pool provides muscle memory, locking and deepening neural pathways in the brain. In the best moments, your brain simply takes over and your body performs the dive almost automatically. Athletes call it a state of flow, an optimal state where you are so mentally absorbed in the process and in control of it, you're operating at a sub-conscious level to reach your peak performance.

But if you think too hard about the process, and ruminate on what could or might go wrong, it is a disaster. Once you have left the board, the dive is very much in motion, and if any parts of it go wrong, you can break bones, crack your ribs, smack your head so you are concussed, or cause permanent damage to your eyes.

Before long, my struggles with my twisting dive, which I started calling my 'demon dive', felt vast.

Often, I physically could not take off from the board. I would count myself in and my feet would remain glued to the platform. Each dive has as much potential to go wrong as the next dive, but for dives without twists, it is much easier to figure your way out of it. Sometimes, when I did eventually get off the board, I had moments when I would lose myself in the air and bail out of the dive, not sure which way up I was or how I would fall or what part of my body would hit the water first. I was like a rag doll, flying through the air and bracing myself for the impact. However hard you train to do something right, when things go wrong human nature simply takes over and there is not that much you can do about it; you are at the mercy of gravity and your brain is telling you to survive. When I think back to those times, all I can remember is the constant and persistent slaps, bangs and smashes, as I landed badly in the water. It was relentless, and the worst thing of all was the knowledge that I would need to pick myself up and go and do it again and again and again until I got it right. Andy, my coach at the time, who I'd been working with for most of my life, was doing his best to help me to try to move through it; he told me steadily and constantly to keep going, to focus on the process and nothing else. He had first seen me dive as a nervous 7-year-old and had witnessed me stumble many, many times, and overcome mental barriers before. When I had struggled as a child, Andy used to tell me to think happy thoughts like the fictional characters Peter Pan and the Darling children had to do in order to fly, so that when I took off, I too would fly. When it went well, that is what it felt like: like I was effortlessly soaring through the air.

But now with my Twister, it no longer felt this way, however hard I tried. The more I obsessed over it, the more it consistently went wrong and the more I panicked about it. I wasn't sure how I would ever get back to competing it properly in international competitions. Like any cycle of panic, I just couldn't break out of it. I felt like I was diving with a ball and chain attached to me.

With each training session where I completed the dive, I would feel great for half an hour and then the terror and panic would set in as I knew I would need to do it again a couple of days later. Even when I was not training that particular dive I worried about it, so I was never present and in the moment. It felt like an awful stop-watch countdown to doing it again, and I would start obsessing about every single thing I could control, like what I was eating, how much I slept and my training times. The littlest things would throw me into a panic. Running late would fill be with anxiety. I became superstitious about walking over drains or under ladders. I had to set my alarm for a certain time; I needed to eat exactly the right thing for breakfast; I would leave at precisely the right time; I couldn't walk over three drains or cracks in the pavements; my music needed to be at a certain volume. If anything was slightly off or didn't run exactly to the precise second, I would feel the adrenalin rush around my body and then convince myself that it meant my Twister would go wrong. I would stand with beads of sweat forming on my lower back and with crazy thoughts whizzing through my mind.

As the months went by after the Olympics, I was at the point where I was so terrified of the Twister that I was pretty much just chucking my body off the side of the board into a twisting motion and hoping for the best. Unsurprisingly, it was a disaster. I despised every second of training. My other dives were going alright and provided some respite from the fear, but my worries about the Twister persisted. I almost overcompensated on the other dives, practising them repetitively until they were perfect. But with no Olympics to train for, I struggled to summon any kind of drive, energy or motivation to continue. Everything was the same: Andy gave me the same set of instructions and guided my training, I was with the same group of divers every day, home was home. But in my mind, there was a fundamental shift.

In the Junior World Championships, which took place in Adelaide, Australia, in October 2012, I only had to compete five dives, so I could leave my Twister out. This was an immense relief and I won the competition beating two of the leading Chinese divers, Yang Jian and Chen Aisen. I know it would probably have been a different story if my twisting dive was on my list. As each day went by, I felt my motivation to try to master my fear of the dive slip away. I just didn't feel I had the strength in me to do it. I felt like I was going crazy.

In 2013, I was put in touch with a new coach, Jane Figueiredo, by Alexei Evangulov, the National Performance Director for the diving squad at British Swimming. British Swimming is the governing body of British aquatic sports, and is responsible for the elite performance of the various disciplines, including diving. As National Performance Director for diving, Alexei's job is to develop and manage the teams to achieve the best results and medal success. He would come and watch me every three weeks or so and he would be at every training camp and competition. Sometimes, he would film us and put together presentations for the team, or individually, about how we could improve our performances. Alexei knew that I wanted to move to London to train at the Aquatics Centre. Andy's home and family were in Plymouth, and he was also training a lot of other athletes there, so he wouldn't be able to support me in London, and my other coach, Peng, had settled in Leeds, so I needed to find someone new to train with.

When Alexei mentioned Jane's name, I was really surprised but excited. She had a formidable reputation working with female Russian springboard divers in America. She was selected because Alexei really liked her technical approach, work ethic and attitude. She is a self-confessed 'dragon' and Alexei felt that Jane could push me to the next level. It was decided that I would travel to Houston, where Jane was living and working, to spend a week there to see how it went. Her becoming my coach would mean a huge change for her and a move to the UK. So much of a successful coach-athlete relationship hinges on successful communication and trust. It needed to be right for both of us.

Of course, I wanted to impress Jane, and for us to get off to a positive start without barriers, so I didn't tell her how I felt about my twisting dive initially. She saw what everyone else had seen at that moment at the Olympics: me striding back up to the board and repeating the dive for a much higher score. The dive was good. But outside of the moment, with its wave of adrenalin, the awful hollowed-out feeling of fear and despondency continued. Jane would never know, just watching me train or compete, how atrocious I was feeling.

The compulsive thoughts had started to wind their way into my life and twist themselves like roots, smothering me, without me realising it. I felt tormented by them. There was one training session in particular that sticks in my mind. It was the first time that I was going to practise my twisting dive with Jane. The day, which fell towards the end of that week, drew closer, like a black cross marked in the ground, and I started to become obsessed about it going well and the ways I might be able to control that. Looking back, it seems almost crazy but I thought that if I did everything perfectly then the day would be alright and my Twister dive would not be a disaster. There was so much noise in my head. I wondered whether training the dive with her could make me re-set my worries, but it just compounded them. Striving to show her how well I could dive seemed to make everything worse. When I eventually got onto the diving board, the dive itself was nothing special but thankfully it had not been awful. After the training session, I went over to her on the poolside. I felt that perhaps if I tried to voice how I was feeling it might make it better.

'I am so terrified of this dive,' I said nervously, trying to confess just how awful I was feeling about it. 'It's also not getting good for me, however much I train. It used to be one of my most consistent dives. I never used to have to think about it.'

'It's fine, don't worry, it will get better . . . We can work on it,' she replied. That's all that was said about it at the time.

I couldn't tell anyone how bad I truly felt about it; I was convinced that they would just tell me to not be crazy. I had just achieved my life-long dream of winning an Olympic medal and there were no other external pressures on me; what didn't I have to feel happy about? How could they possibly understand? Even I was struggling to comprehend what was happening and why I was feeling so anxious.

I slept badly and constantly dreamed about falling. I would always be at the bottom of the ladders on random diving boards that were not like the ones at any pool I trained at. The ladders were strange, winding and narrow, and it would seem an almost impossible climb to the top. When the board was within my sight, I would slip and fall into the abyss and see the world flashing by, just like in my dives. I would never land but just wake up with my heart hammering, sometimes shouting and thrashing about in my sleep. I felt constantly drained and mentally wrung out, like my brain had been through the washing machine on a spin cycle. I knew I needed to keep going. I had experienced having more bad days than good days before in my diving, but this took it to another level.

The problem came to a head at the National Championships in Southend in January 2014. The competition came after a couple of periods of time off, and physically I wasn't in my best shape. I had gone travelling around the world for six weeks and then I'd taken some time off for Christmas in Plymouth with my own family. I was also in the middle of filming the TV show *Splash!* for ITV and had travelled from Luton the night before after filming. Jane was in the UK; I had trained with her for that initial week, and then a month in Houston in 2013, and it had gone well, but I was hoping to make a good impression while she was watching my first competition. To top all that off, Lance, who I had started dating around a year earlier and who I was starting to get really serious about, was also in the audience watching for the first time. It felt like the perfect storm of pressure, and my Twister was right in the eye of it.

This was a competition between British divers that I had taken part in for well over a decade. I knew all eyes were on me. There was an expectation to win; it was in every cheer, every autograph that I signed, and in every smiling face I saw. With any national competition, it is not a case of being OK with fourth place. Why would I not win when I had competed and won against the best divers in the world? It's hard to feel the same sort of adrenalin that you feel at an international competition at national competitions, though, so there is a lot of space for sloppy diving. No one could understand the pressure and expectation there was to dive well.

In the morning, I had competed my Twister in the prelims and it was a disaster, and whilst I was still in the lead, it was not by the margin I was used to. I had thrown myself off the diving board and chucked my body around. It was ugly and felt like a mess. My form was deteriorating fast and I didn't know how I could claw it back. I knew how quickly things could go badly wrong.

Getting ready to perform that dive for the final of the competition, I remember standing at the back of the board and just falling apart. I was shaking and sobbing. I tried to inhale but my breath felt short and shallow and I was unsteady on my feet, with tingling hands and numb legs. The physical manifestation of fear and panic was horrendous but my thoughts were worse. At that moment, I hated myself, how I felt, and my internal dialogue.

There used to be a time that diving was fairly niche and anyone could turn up for the competition and buy tickets to watch on the day. Now these home competitions would sell out in just a few hours. The stands and poolside seats would be packed with everyone from huge diving fans that came to a lot of my competitions through to locals in Southend, looking for some weekend entertainment and to see an Olympian in action. I told myself I was going to be a huge embarrassment to everyone. That I would land flat and make a fool of myself. That people had come to watch me and that all they would feel was disappointment. I loathed what I had become and was humiliated by my thoughts. I didn't care about myself or what I did. It felt like everything had spiralled out of control. Most of all, my inability to speak to anyone about what I was experiencing meant that I felt so, so alone.

Jane came over to the board and she tried her best to say the right thing but our relationship was a new one and I imagine she felt confused.

'It's going to be OK,' she said. 'You've been doing it fine in training.'

'I know I have to get up and do it,' I muttered between sobs, feeling deeply ashamed and embarrassed by my outburst but unable to stop the tears. 'But everything is telling me I can't.'

Andy came over from where he was sitting on the poolside, watching the drama unfold. He was there with his divers from Plymouth and he attempted to talk me down from the ledge.

'Just concentrate on the process and getting through the dives,' he told me. 'Take each dive at a time. Don't overthink it.'

'I can go one dive at a time, but I'm going to have to get to that dive at some point in all this. I have to do it in front of all these people. It's not going to be good.'

I knew it was going to go wrong; it was just a case of how spectacularly wrong it could go. Of course, at that stage my anxious mindset was not improving matters and, by that point, I did not believe that that dive would ever go well again.

All coaches were also divers in a previous life, so they did understand the fear that I felt to a degree, but Andy's words didn't really register. Somehow I got myself up to the top of the board. Ultimately, in those very long seconds and minutes, I knew I had to make a decision about whether I wanted to be the guy crying at the bottom of the board or not; I knew I had to complete the dive at some point or pull out of the competition, and I am not a quitter, so there was no alternative. In the end, I made it off the board, but not without a mental struggle. Needless to say, I dived badly for the rest of that competition. At the time there were not many UK divers competing at the same level as me, and so the fact that I barely scraped a gold medal meant that I left the pool feeling pretty low. I knew I needed to just single-mindedly keep going, but it felt almost impossible to see a way through.

We pushed through the year, trying many different ways to overcome my fears. I was lucky that I had a sports psychologist, Kate, who I had worked with for a long time and was able to open up to. We tried to unpick the knots of what was going on in my head and attempted to get to the root of it. Whilst London 2012 played an enormous role in my panic, I started to realise that my twisting dive was one that I had always deeply feared, back to when I was young and I'd had to persevere with it then. As a child, I had progressed through the ranks and dived from ten metres from quite a young age. I never really loved the springboard in the same way as the high boards because I didn't feel the same sense of excitement and adrenalin. The higher up the platforms I moved, the more enthusiastic I felt about diving in general. I was naturally athletic and it was a fit for my skills; one of my favourite party tricks at family weddings and parties was crossing the dancefloor on my hands. Diving just clicked for me. I always loved the feeling of weightlessness and exhilaration when I was diving from the higher boards. Despite this, the nerves were never far from the surface.

Officially, you are not supposed to dive from that board until the age of 12 because of the risk to growing joints, but

I completed my first dive from ten metres when I was just 8. I had completed all the dives I could on the lower boards, and I needed a challenge to keep me focused, so it had made sense for me to dive from there. This was also when I started doing 'optionals', which are the dives without difficulty limit, that I started to complete at senior competitions, and I could score more highly from the top board. Then came another problem: after mastering a dive, I would grow, and suddenly my legs would be longer than I was used to, or my arms had grown, and so every time I would get into a tuck or pike, everything was a bit different and I would hurt myself. As a youngster, I quickly learned how easy it was to get a serious injury. On one occasion, I did a warm-up dive off the poolside and I clipped my head. I got out of the water with crimson blood pooling on the floor around me. I landed flat many times, and remember one time where my legs had grown so my feet had clipped the old board in Plymouth, and I had stormed straight out of the pool and hidden in my dad's van. There were many occasions that I would burst into tears and refuse to try new dives, and around the age of 11, I didn't dive off the ten-metre board for almost a whole year because I kept feeling like I was losing myself in the air and I couldn't phys-ically make myself jump from the platform. This was put down to Lost Movement Syndrome, a term applied in sports like gymnastics, diving or trampolining, where athletes are unable to perform a movement that they could previously manage. The mental pathways my brain had relied on to navigate the dive had become flooded with fear and panic. I had spoken to Andy and various other athletes and psychologists about it, who had reassured me that with perseverance, patience and practice, I would get over it. Andy encouraged me to take it right back to basics and not rush it. He later told me that he could see I had talent and potential and was determined for me to find the fun and love for the sport again. I did get through it and I had to adopt a resilient mindset, where I persevered, even though some days were awful and I felt like I had taken many steps back rather than forwards. It had been painstakingly slow work, but in the end I managed to dive back off the top board and regain some confidence.

So, I'd had moments like this before, when I felt overwhelmed, and had tried to break my dives back down and build them back up again slowly, move by move. I had tried so hard to do this, but the problem with my Twister felt far, far bigger than anything I had experienced before.

It was Kate who first brought up the medical term, Post Traumatic Stress Disorder. When she mentioned that PTSD could be behind the emotions I'd been feeling around my dive I was really shocked. I thought she was wrong; how could I have suffered trauma from falling into water? From something that I love to do? How could that be at the root of my panic and obsessive thoughts, when I'd seen so many stories of people suffering it who had come back from tours of

Afghanistan? I believe that this is one reason why mental health is so hard to talk about and understand. It is so easy to just think that you would have no reason to feel a certain way, or you had no justification for feeling bad, or you simply are not the type of person who would suffer. Why would I experience PTSD when I had so many great things going on in my life? I asked myself this question constantly. But the more Kate talked, the more I started to understand that whilst I hadn't been to war, been in an awful car accident, or experienced something tangibly awful from the outside, trauma can come in many forms. Any event that has provoked a sense of profound fear or distress can cause PTSD. I started to accept what had happened, and that mental health problems can happen to anyone at any time. Like physical health, no one is infallible from suffering from mental health setbacks. I was no different from anyone else.

We tried to start to unravel what had gone wrong and why I felt like I did, so I could try to begin the long process of recovery and overcome it. A large part of this was accepting the problem so I could keep going. We attempted various treatments to make me feel better, including EMDR or Eye Movement Desensitisation Reprogramming, which is a technique to aid the processing of information and memories. She also suggested that I practise various breathing, visualisation and meditation processes, but I fought against it and was convinced it would not help. I told her it was a load of crap and would never work – why would breathing differently stop me feeling so bad? Back then, mindfulness and meditation were less mainstream than they are now, and I could not understand how taking some deep breaths and focusing on being in the present moment would make any difference to healing the trauma I had suffered. I half-heartedly tried to give it a go and sat for ten minutes trying to ignore the many thoughts rattling like trains through my brain, but I never really committed to it. Whatever we did my fear persisted, like set concrete that weighed heavily around me. I was clueless about the benefits that these sorts of practices could have.

It took me some time to come to terms with what had happened at the Olympics, why I felt like I did and why it had been so traumatic for me, and I had to do this before I could even begin to move forwards. I began to recognise how hard I was trying to push my fear away and how this simply made my anxiety tighten its grip on me. The more I attempted to block it out, the tighter the vice held and the more it grew. The different processes Kate had suggested were all rooted in re-living the moment as closely as I could, so it could become smaller and less important in my mind. I began to see that I needed to hit it head on and acknowledge my feelings, but whatever I tried, my feelings toward the Twister simply did not get better. The fear still sat like a monster on my shoulder.

In coaching, Jane and I had touched on the idea of a different twisting dive, but I was scared that I would experience the same problem and hit the same wall, wherever the twist was within the dive, or whether it was simply in another direction. I ruminated on everything that went wrong with my back-twister and thought that I would simply transfer that fear to any new twisting dive. The twisting dive only needs to have a twist in it – it could be forwards, backwards, inwards or reverse. Whilst every other elite diver performed the Twister as it is, there was nothing in the rulebook saying that I couldn't compete another dive. Jane showed me different dives but I wasn't convinced. I thought it was way too dramatic to start thinking about another dive, when every single other athlete competed the same one. To learn a new dive from scratch would be a massive undertaking and would take hundreds of hours of practice.

But I had also recognised that I'd been trying to persevere with my Twister ever since the 2012 Olympics, and I was now starting to consider that I might need to make a change. Without it, I wasn't sure I could keep going, while looking after my own mental well-being and progressing in my sport. There is a time and a place to persevere and push through. What's more, perseverance is not just about 'sticking with it'; sometimes it is about solving a problem by thinking more laterally. I started to come round to the idea that a new approach and a new dive could help me.

We found a resolution in 2014 after the World Cup in Shanghai, where I missed out on a podium finish, coming fourth, and I had flown back to Houston to train with Jane again. She came over to the poolside one day after training.

'I've been thinking. Take a look at this,' she said.

She took out her phone and showed me a blurry YouTube clip. It was part of an old Cirque Du Soleil show and three performers were on a Russian swing, a type of swing that is able to rotate 360 degrees and allows acrobats to gain enough momentum and height to perform tricks into the air, landing either on dry land or in the water. In this show, the acrobats swung back and forth a few times to gather momentum until the board was swinging in a high arc, before the front-facing performer leaped off at the peak of the arc into the air, doing a front three and a half somersault dive with one twist piked, before landing gracefully in the water.

'I know it's a circus trick but I think this could be your twisting dive,' she said. 'I've been looking at this and studying it. I think this is the way we have to go. We have to put the twist at the end.'

'Could I even do that?' I asked. 'Is it even possible?'

'I've seen someone do it on a springboard before. I don't see why not.'

We needed to think outside the box. I knew it would mean hours and hours of painstaking and detailed work, with no reference point. No one in the world had competed this dive before. It felt like a massive risk but this was one that I knew I needed to take.

'OK, let's go for it.'

Jane and I started to work on my new twisting dive. For a while, we just experimented and tried different things. I started practising from the five-metre board and I had looked at twisting first and then rolling into a pike shape, so it was slightly different from what the Cirque du Soleil video was showing. It made the dive really hard because fighting against the G-force to get into the pike shape is really difficult. I ended up hurting my thumb because it was too low finishing. Then I tried doing one somersault, then flicking out, then going back into a pike shape. But still the G-force was too high. While we are spinning around in a dive, we go through a similar amount of G-force to fighter pilots, so changing direction is really difficult. In the end, the only way we thought it would be possible would be doing two and a half somersaults first and then flicking out into the twist during the third and final somersault, to make the complete dive three and a half somersaults with one twist.

There is an official table with all the different dives, and a formula to work out the degree of difficulty of each dive. I needed any new dive to be the same degree of difficulty or higher than the original Twister, so I could gain enough points and not put myself at a disadvantage. The degree of difficulty is a rating based on the number of somersaults, twists, and specific details of the execution. We worked that out first, to see it if was even worth it. Each dive is awarded a score out of 10 and all elements of the dive are taken into account, including the approach, take off, elevation, execution and entry. The two highest and two lowest scores are dropped and then the dive's degree of difficulty is multiplied by the sum of the judges' scores to obtain a final score for the dive. If it was as little as even 0.1 degree of difficulty less, it would not be worth it as I would not be able to beat the best divers.

On paper, my new dive – which we named the Firework – was a much harder dive and the stakes were much higher, so we thought it might gain a higher degree of difficulty and more points. But in the end, both the Twister and the Firework have a degree of difficulty of 3.6 – enough points to score over 100 if the dive is executed well.

To learn any new dive, we broke it all the way down to practise the separate components before gradually putting them together and building it up to the complete dive. We tried it in the harness over the trampoline, then off the dry board into the foam pit, then out of the harness into the pit, then from the different boards at the pool, working out how exactly I would fit all the movements into the dive. It was slow, repetitive and painstaking work.

We practise many of our dives off the three-metre spring-board. With the springboard you can benefit from the energy generated during your approach to the end of the board by doing 'hurdle steps' or using 'double bouncing' – basically, approaching the board lifting one leg and taking off using both, or using the board like a trampoline and doing a two footed bounce. I practised this dive with a double bounce to get the maximum height from the board, so that I was able to do the twists and somersaults on both the way up and the way down. The springboard gives me the momentum to perform all the moves that I need to, and is often used in training to take away the difficult balance issues that are associated with a one-legged 'hurdle' approach. On the ten-metre board, through your movement, you need to provide this momentum yourself to complete all the movements in the space between taking off and landing in the water. You can also only do a certain number of dives from the ten-metre platform in one training session, because the overall impact on your body is immense. With the springboard you are much closer to the water, so when it goes wrong, the force of impact is less. The difficult part of the dive, the twisting part, is at the end, and I couldn't practise that without doing the start of the dive, so we had to find enough momentum and elevation for me to do that. For all my other dives, I could complete parts of them from the five-metre platform, so this meant I was learning this dive in a slightly different way. For example, while I could do a back three and a half somersaults piked from ten metres, I could only do a two and a half somersaults piked from five metres. But because the twist was at the end of the Firework, I always had to practise it from ten metres. I always knew that I would have to do a running take off because with forward-spinning dives, it is the only way to generate enough momentum and force.

Previously when I had learned a new dive, I would study videos of other people competing it but we had no reference point. Even when Leon Taylor invented the back two and a half somersaults and two and a half twists, and he was the first person to compete it in international competition, the difference was that people were doing a back two and a half somersaults and one and a half twists, so he had just added an extra twist to what was already out there. My running forwards twisting dive was a complete unknown.

When I first went up to ten metres to do the dive, I had no idea how it would fall. Was I ever going to make it? What would I do if it went wrong? Would I have enough time? It felt like we were experimenting the whole time, with variables such as how fast to take off, how much to lean forwards versus standing up, how much jump versus rotation; there were so many unknowns, and no way of learning without simply doing it.

My first attempt at the Firework was scary but exciting. I don't remember every nanosecond of it but I do remember completing all the separate elements in the right order, lining up in time, and landing on my head. I had done it. It felt amazing.

I was starting to build up to the idea of competing the Firework in competitions. There was a renewed sense of purpose in my diving. I went through the same repetitive practices of rehearsing parts of the dive and then working on it from the top board. I had to grit my teeth because I still struggled, and had days when the dive did not go well. I had to remind myself to see each dive as an individual event, so if I did one bad Firework dive, that did not mean that it was not going well in general. When I struggled, I gave myself something that I looked forward to at the end of each day. When it felt hard, I reminded myself of the special meal, outing or event that I had planned. I knew I had to keep pushing through because there was no alternative. I had to keep a cool head and continue working hard, trusting that I would get where I needed to be. I had to focus on the process. On the days that it went well, I felt like I was flying again.

One of the first competitions where I competed my Firework dive was as part of the FINA World Series in 2015. FINA (Fédération Internationale de Natation) is the governing body of diving. The World Series is a series of annual competitions that happen across the world every year for divers from all countries. Most of the divers are previous Olympic medallists or World Champions, having qualified in the top eight in the previous year's major event. The competition was in London, and I was back in front of a home crowd. During the same competition the previous year in 2014, my performance had gone badly and I had been placed fifth. One of my biggest rivals, the Chinese diver Yang Jian, had scored an incredible world record with the highest score for an individual dive of all time. The Chinese are always my biggest rivals, and can be frightening in their consistency and aptitude. They train at phenomenally high standards, training in the pool almost all day, every day, and spur each other on with an entrenched sense of competition between them. The fact this happened in London, where I worked and trained, and in front of a home crowd, made his success more glaring and pronounced in my head. I had plodded along in that competition with my shitty Twister, knowing it would not go well. I had known that something had to change, if I was ever going to be the best in the world again.

On that day, a year later, it all started to click back into place again. I had been diving more consistently and my Firework was going well. My friends and family were watching and I was eager to get out there and compete against the best. I knew I could. My Firework, which I performed second in my list, went brilliantly, scoring 99 points, the second-highest score I had received for it. My back three and a half somersaults piked had scored well over 100, and I beat Yang and the other Chinese diver, Qiu Bo, by a decent margin. The Chinese divers often dominate the leader board, but on that day I had triumphed. They are beatable, and I had shown this again. You can go into any competition hoping to do well, but if you don't believe you can win, then it's never going to happen. After months of doubting myself, I knew on that day that I had a chance to be a winner again. I had persevered and found a route through.

We all have struggles and hurdles to navigate, and this was a colossal mountain for me to climb, but I had done it. I was coming back down the other side. I started to believe in myself and my ability again. It felt like it had been a long time coming.

Since then, I have learned more about mindfulness and being more present in the moment and this has really informed my diving. Now I have a finely honed routine at every competition. When there are around five or six divers left before my turn, I will get a coaching comment from Jane. I get to the bottom of the board and take a sip of my drink. I walk up to the three-metre platform and another diver will go. I then move to the five-metre board, where I cover my eyes with my shammy and visualise the dive in my head. Then, as another diver jumps, I move to the seven-metre, and that is when I do my physical run-through of my arm swing, my shape, and how I come out of the dive. I close my eyes, feel my feet on the platform, and think about what I can feel, hear, smell and taste, to ground me in the moment. Then I do ten very deep breaths in and out to try to bring my heart rate down.

Then, feeling calm, and in the moment, I walk up to the ten-metre board and complete my dive.

I wish I had started learning about the importance of breathing earlier; we are never too young to learn more about how we can use simple breathing techniques and different mediation practices to help our minds. I was once told, 'Fear is excitement without breathing', which really drove home the importance of breathing exercises in my diving, to the point that they are now part of every dive I complete. I started using an app called Headspace every day for ten minutes, which teaches meditation and mindfulness through guided audio sessions. This allows me to find a calm space within myself, no matter what is going on around me – whether I am at home, training, at competitions or doing other work. I have found it incredibly helpful for blocking the noise out when I am in competitions, but it could also be helpful for a job interview or a stressful social situation. Stress from anything can find its way into your sport and performance. With meditation, you can bring yourself back to the moment and it is an incredible tool to have in your armoury. It is time just for me, and I find it really empowering.

When I first started trying to meditate, I found it almost impossible to concentrate on the process; I would think about when it would finish, what was for dinner, whether I should put a wash on, why I was wasting my time. But when I made the commitment to just do it for ten minutes a day and be present, it started to work. As I started to feel more centred, it was a euphoric feeling and allowed me to feel much calmer around my twisting dive and my diving in general. The fear of a dive going badly wrong is still, of course, never that far away but as my career has progressed, I have learned more about how I can manage my worries, so they never become all-consuming.

For me, the lesson in perseverance and innovation around my twisting dive was about understanding the bigger picture and where I wanted and needed to end up. I always knew what I needed to do, but for a long time I couldn't quite see how to get there. There were many up and downs and days when I felt like I had taken twenty steps backwards, and other days when I made inches of progress forwards. Although I felt like I was failing for a long time, once I had turned a corner, I could see the light at the end of the tunnel. Every athlete is always, always learning. In creating a new dive, Jane and I had ripped up the rulebook, and I could finally understand where I was going again.

COURAGE

In March 2013, Nickelodeon asked me to fly out to Los Angeles as a guest of The Nickelodeon Kids' Choice Awards where I had won the 'Favourite UK Sports Star' category. Whilst I was in LA, I had an invitation to dinner from a friend, who told me to bring a couple of my friends; they said that they would bring a couple of theirs. I took some of the Nickelodeon team with me. We were about forty minutes late to dinner because the Nickelodeon guys had spent ages at the bar; I remember trying to cajole them away from their drinks and feeling really flustered arriving at the table, where everyone was already sitting and waiting for us. My eyes were immediately drawn to a man with huge broad shoulders, sitting in a corner seat at one end of the table. He was wearing a thin red hoodie and a worn leather jacket. Masses of sandy blonde hair partially obscured his eyes; as my own lingered on him for perhaps a few seconds too long, I saw a smile appear. Immediately, I thought, 'Who is that?'

I had no idea about who Lance was or what he did, and after a few seconds it seemed that he didn't know anything about me either (he later admitted that he had watched me at the Olympics, but just didn't let on to me at the time). We made awful small talk about what happens in the Olympic village and how it might make a great romcom. Everyone at the table was talking about TV, films and screenwriters. I got the sense that he was a big deal and started fumbling with my phone to Google him at the table – this was not something I would ever normally do, but I usually make a point of finding out who I will be meeting, and what they do, so I'm prepared. It's important for conversation starters and I didn't want to make a fool of myself or, even worse, embarrass any-one else. I clocked quickly that he was a screenwriter, film-maker and Academy Award winner, and a big LGBTQ+ campaigner. Later on that evening, my friend who invited me told me to guess Lance's age, and I thought he was probably about 28. When he told me that Lance was twenty years older than me, I didn't believe him. Even when I clocked his birth year on Wikipedia, I thought it was wrong. I was intrigued by him and it felt like the chemistry was instant. As the dinner progressed, I kept looking at him and he kept catching my eye, which was awkward at times because I just couldn't look away. Whenever he looked at me and saw me staring, I would look away, feeling as though I had been caught.

After dinner, the group went to have a few drinks and Lance's assistant asked me if Lance could have my number. I punched my number into the notes in his phone and added an emoji winking face. I hoped that was enough to convey my interest – he later said that no straight man puts a winky face after their number!

Sure enough, the next morning when I reached for my phone, there was a text message saying how great it was to meet me. I felt an unfamiliar surge of butterflies.

That evening we met again and spent six hours talking. Because I was still not 21 and I couldn't drink legally in public, he came over to my hotel, bringing a couple of Diet Cokes from the In-N-Out Burger next door, and we made some drinks with the miniatures in my mini bar. We bypassed the small talk this time, and very quickly chatted on a much deeper level. My dad, Rob, had died of a brain tumour in 2011 when he was just 40, and Lance had lost his brother Marcus to cancer in 2012, so we talked about our respective losses. He had won an Academy Award in 2008 for Best Original Screenplay for the biopic, *Milk*, about the life of the assassinated gay rights activist Harvey Milk. He said that winning the Oscar was amazing, a whirlwind-like two weeks when you're everything. And then it was over. Back to work. But it wasn't just about work anymore, it was about working to a level that could win more Oscars. That resonated so much with me. He had also been at the top of his game, and so I felt that he understood what I was going through: now I had won an Olympic medal, I needed to stay at that altitude. We both knew that after the highest of career highs could come the lowest of lows.

After hours of talking, I asked him if he had ever been taught to dive.

I stood up and said, 'Clasp your hands above your head – that's how we enter the water when we dive.' As he did, I leaned in and kissed him.

Suddenly, everything felt joined up. It made sense. Whilst I had had relationships before, I guess it had never felt completely right and, until that moment, I couldn't quite see why. I thought I'd been in love before but it was nothing compared to this.

I very quickly fell head over heels for Lance. I felt lovestruck – we spoke, FaceTimed and messaged each other constantly; I couldn't get him out of my head. It was intense and my feelings just grew and grew.

When I got back from LA, the first person I told about what had happened was my friend, Sophie. We had been on a night out to some bars in Plymouth and were eating pizza back at my house. We had both had quite a lot to drink, and I guess at that point I was never going to tell anyone about my feelings when I was completely sober.

'I'm just going to come out and say this now in the hope that you or both of us will've forgotten we had this conversation by the morning,' I muttered.

She looked at me, confused.

'So, I met someone in LA. I think I've met the person I want to be with.'

'Oh great, what's she like?'

'Well, it's a guy.'

'Oh right,' she replied. She didn't even bat an eyelid.

'Is that all you are going say?'

'Yeah, I don't care. I'm happy for you.'

She gave me a hug and we continued tucking into our pepperoni pizza.

It felt good that someone knew, and there was someone I could talk to about Lance. I felt for the first time that I could be myself. I didn't have to hide away like some sort of hermit crab.

Lance was, and still is, a real workaholic. He never took any holidays or days off. With a previous boyfriend, the best he had managed was the commitment of a weekend away; he left on the Friday evening and by the Saturday morning, he was freaking out that he didn't have his laptop with him, so he had to go home. So, it was quite a leap of faith to start dating someone who lived over 5,000 miles and an eleven-hour flight away, and with an eight-hour time difference to boot. But we made it work.

We planned to meet up around my nineteenth birthday in May 2013, a few weeks after we had met. He told me he was scouting for locations in London for one of the projects he was working on. When I picked him up from the airport, I felt exactly as I knew I would: completely besotted. I couldn't take my eyes off him. We went straight back to the hotel and got changed to go out for drinks and dinner for my birthday with my friends. After three lychee martinis, I was telling all of them and anyone else who would listen that he was my boyfriend. It might sound like a cliché but it happened quickly and I knew he was 'the one' for me. We spent a few days in London and whilst I did some media and sponsorship work, Lance went out taking pictures for his film project and we met in the evenings. We went to the Oxo Tower one night for dinner, for our first proper date. I didn't know London that well, but had been for dinner there for my eighteenth birthday with my friends and family, and the views of London are pretty special. We spent a wonderful evening getting to know each other and played a game where we would ask each other questions and had to answer truthfully. He asked if I would be his boyfriend; I guess we both wanted to make sure we were reading the situation correctly. Then the following day, he told me that he loved me. I felt the same. I loved the fact he was so sensitive, protective and amazingly supportive. I had unwavering trust in him. We still go back to the Oxo Tower sometimes now, and it feels special because it is our first date spot.

I had to go back to Plymouth as I had a birthday party planned. Lance had not committed to coming with me when he first came over to the UK, but things had gone so amazingly that he sat by my side on the train back to my home town.

Back in Plymouth, we decided to go on a bike ride along the Camel Trail that runs twelve miles from Padstow to Bodmin in Cornwall. As we cycled along in the sun, we chatted about everything and broke all the rules about what you are and are not supposed to talk about so early on. Family has always been immensely important to me, and I have always known that I have wanted to get married and have children. When I saw my future, a family was always at the heart of it. I had been buying children's clothes since I was about 17, and had a whole drawer full of little tops and romper suits from my travels. When I travelled to various countries with my diving I would spot cute little outfits in the airport shops and not know when I would be passing again, so I would buy them and stash them away. By then, I had a whole drawer of clothes and it really mattered to me that whoever I was with for the long-term also wanted those things. I appreciate this is unusual for a man, and I was young, but it was something that I enjoyed. I pictured my future and there was always a baby and children in it. I wanted to be a hands-on father, like my dad had been for me.

'Do you think you'd like to get married?' Lance asked me.

'Of course. I'd love to.' I grinned as I responded.

Lance is a founding board member of the American Foundation for Equal Rights and was at the forefront of fighting for marriage equality in the US. Legislation to allow same-sex marriage in the UK was going through Parliament at the time.

I then went one step further.

'And do you think you'd like to have kids in the future?'

'I'd love that,' he told me.

We then named our kids and started to map out what the future could look like. It was clear we both wanted the same things in life.

Before he went home, we went to the local garden centre and Lance bought me a barbecue for my birthday. We invited my mum and friends over and cooked up a feast. Lance made burgers from scratch and grilled them on the barbecue with crumbled blue cheese in the middle.

When it was just the two of us in the kitchen, I decided to ask Mum what she thought of Lance. 'He makes a great burger,' she replied. I had to agree with her.

'Well Lance and I, we are together,' I told her.

She paused for a moment, looking a bit confused. I could see her mind whirring but then she smiled.

'That's great, if you are happy, I am happy,' she told me, giving me a familiar, warm hug.

She had a lot of questions about it, including how it worked in the bedroom – I told her we might need more to drink before we got on to that!

Everyone loved Lance; he slotted into our group of friends and just got on with everyone.

But I did not expect my close family's reaction to my relationship with Lance to be replicated if I came out to the wider sporting community. Homophobic and transphobic language still pervades sport, which is dominated by heteronormative men. This was even more pronounced eight years ago; in 2013 there were virtually no gay sports stars who had been brave enough to come out. The Welsh former-professional rugby player Gareth Thomas had come out in 2009, but that was at the end of his career, and I wasn't aware of many more people at all. There must have been countless more out there, with boyfriends or girlfriends that only those closest to them were aware of. I didn't know any sportsman who had come out in the middle of their career rather than towards the end of it.

Growing up, I'd always known I was different from other kids. In my primary school, I was one of five boys in a class of thirty. I always got on well with everyone, was a class clown, and was always proud of the fact that I had 'two boyfriends and three girlfriends'.

When you're a child, there is never any right or wrong way to be having relationships; when you are the age of 5 or 6 you are able to just be yourself. There is wonderful innocence and acceptance. As I went through my primary years, I didn't feel the same as my friends; it didn't matter because I was so invested in my sport and was travelling around, but this in turn further enhanced our differences. Many of them didn't understand my love of diving. They didn't get that I wanted to spend five hours in the pool after school, rather than go to the cinema for the 9 p.m. showing if I had to get up at 6 a.m. the next day for training. They couldn't understand that going to the shopping centre on a Saturday wasn't really my idea of fun. There was something special at that time about going to diving training and being able to be me. It provided another focus away from school and any sort of teenage peer pressure. It was a space like home, a safe haven where I was accepted. My home life with my parents and two younger brothers, William and Ben, was so supportive, I never questioned too deeply the fact that I didn't fit in.

When I went to secondary school, I had a larger group of friends and some of them had older siblings; it was only when I was with them that I started to understand that 'gay' wasn't just an insult that was thrown around, or a way of describing something that was lame or a bit bad, but a definition of sexuality. I think I always knew that I had feelings for men as well as women, but for a long time I thought that everyone was attracted to both sexes. Like many things in adolescence, everything started to click into place and I began to understand that there was a name for what I was feeling. I felt alienated from my friends and as though my feelings were something I should hide or not talk about; at that time, it was simply not seen as a good thing to be gay. From the age of about 13 or 14, I dated girls, and I never really felt like I was missing out. It felt like the only people who were out were the people who could not possibly hide their sexuality.

Going to the Beijing Olympics in 2008 when I was 14 isolated me even further from my peer group. My sexuality was less of a focus for the school bullies; they were more interested in pointing out how little I wore when I was diving, and how the pictures of me were always practically naked. 'Diver Boy' and 'Speedo Boy' became frequent taunts in the musty school corridors, and I was often tackled to the ground or had stuff thrown at me in the classroom. My bags would be emptied over the floor, or the bigger kids would ask me how much my legs were insured for, so they could break them. I had the staunch support of my parents and my friends, but this kind of behaviour seemed to be accepted by everyone, even me back then. The school gave me an empty classroom to go to with my friends during the breaks, to avoid the worst of it, but even this was seen as some sort of special treatment, and soon it felt like almost the whole school was making jokes at my expense. The nerves really kicked in when I started to feel physically threatened. When we were outside the class-room, my friends would fan out and try to form a protective ring around me like a human shield, so the bullies couldn't get to me. I would pretend that it did not bother me and laugh it off where I could, being the class clown. But deep down, I was scared. I would head to training in the evenings, after bad days at school, and feel the anxiety fall away with each dive. It allowed me to not think about it.

One day when the bell went and I was leaving that empty classroom, I was tackled by a burly older kid and I fell and landed awkwardly on my wrist, causing it to swell up. I had to stop my training for the week to let it recover. I was frustrated and upset. My parents were forced to pull me out of school and look at other education options; they had been to the school many times about it and felt like they were running out of options.

Internally, my struggles at school and to fit in gave me an even stronger motivation to focus on my diving and excel at my sport. I thought that if I worked a bit harder and proved to everyone I could be a success because I was different from them, then that would prove the bullies wrong. In this way, I felt that I could overcompensate for not quite fitting the mould.

As I moved more into the public eye my sexuality and relationships became more of a focus, and the media seemed obsessed with my love life. I was always asked, 'Do you have a girlfriend?' to which I responded that diving was my number one focus, which wasn't a lie. I had girlfriends, and went through periods of dating, but it was never that serious.

When the same question came after I had met Lance, I never felt there was a right time to say, 'No, but I do have a boyfriend . . .' I knew how trustworthy my friends were, so for me the worry about the general public finding out never felt like a big issue initially. When Lance and I went out to dinner together, I would often ask Sophie to come with us, so people didn't see the two of us and start to question the nature of the relationship.

But the more time went on, the more I started thinking and worrying about it. I wanted to tell the truth and be myself, but I genuinely thought that if people knew I was gay, then my life wouldn't be as I knew it. I had started to be sponsored by big brands, like Visa and adidas, quite early on in my career, and as soon as I earned to a certain level, I no longer received any money from British Diving. I was worried that if I came out, these brands would stop supporting me, so how I would continue diving without funding was a huge concern. I thought it would be the end of any sponsorship deals I had, any TV career that I might have in the future; I thought my fans would hate me and the parents of young divers would be horrified, or maybe they would discourage their children from diving because of me. I thought it would literally be the end of the world and that people would shout at me in the street.

I didn't have any template about how I should come out or what I should say. Matthew Mitcham from Australia, who had won the ten-metre Olympic gold in 2008, was openly gay, and I read that he had come out ahead of that Olympic Games in the *Sydney Morning Herald*. I was nervous to do the same because I did not want my words being changed. Whilst diving was very inclusive and accepting of differences, as I've said, the world of sport as a whole wasn't. The reality was that it was pretty homophobic, and it was always safer to stay quiet than to speak out. And outside of competing in the UK, I would need to take part in competitions in countries where homosexuality was illegal. But I wanted to be strong and not hide that side of myself. And most importantly, I never wanted anyone to say that I was a liar.

There was never any pressure from Lance for me to come out and tell everyone. He told me to do and say what I wanted at my own pace. He said it was not something I should rush into, and everything should happen in my own time.

I took the idea of coming out to my agent at the time, who was clearly very nervous about it. At the time we were filming the second series of the TV show *Splash!* and he suggested holding off until the series had wrapped. When I had told him a few months previously that Lance was coming to visit for my birthday – at that point he didn't know we were together – he had warned me to be careful about being photo-graphed going in and out of clubs with him, because Lance is known as being a big LGBTQ+ rights activist.

My agent told me to think about it, and that he would give

it some more thought too, but I could tell from the way he spoke and his body language that he was never ever behind the idea, and that he never really understood, or tried to understand, how I felt. I guess as the managing director of a big sports management group, unsurprisingly, he had probably never had to manage a situation like that before.

I started to become increasingly paranoid. If people were judging me for spending time with Lance, then what would they say if they knew we were in a relationship?

The final straw came during an interview in September 2013, when a journalist kept asking me about my gay following and why I thought it was so big. She just wouldn't let it drop, arguing that people thought I was gay and asking me what I thought about that.

'It wouldn't bother me in the slightest what people thought,' I replied. 'But I can understand why I have a massive gay following – I spend most of my life half naked in trunks on a diving board showing off my bare chest.'

My heart was racing. I tried to turn the attention back to my sport, adding, 'I just think about my diving. If people think I am gay, or that I don't focus on my diving enough and go out too much, there is always going to be an opinion – and if I worry too much, that's when my diving goes down-hill.'

I didn't want to lie, but equally, I wasn't going to tell a pushy journalist the truth because she was trying to force it out of me. I was starting to worry too much and the whole thing was taking up so much time and energy, it was interfering with everything. It felt exhausting and like I was now starting to live a lie, not of my own making.

The next day the headline read, 'Tom Daley: I am NOT gay – but I don't care if you think I am.'

I did not say that, and seeing it written in this way made me so angry. I just didn't understand how that could happen, and how my words could be twisted. My initial reaction was that I wanted to hit back and insist on a correction, but of course, as one of my management team at the time pointed out, the only thing I could say in that situation was that I was gay.

I started to feel so stressed about it, and I knew that I was using valuable mental energy worrying about what people were saying about me all the time. I knew that it was time to speak out.

Despite everyone's reservations, I decided that it was time for me to come out; I had fallen head over heels in love with the most wonderful man and it had got to the point where I no longer wanted to hide away.

I needed to have the courage to step forwards and be open about my private life, whatever the repercussions of that. To calm myself down whenever I started to feel panicked, I started to rationalise my sexuality in my head. If I came out as gay or bisexual, I would still be able to stand on the diving board and dive off it. I feel like people always want labels to define someone and put them in a box, be it gay, lesbian, bisexual, transgender, or whatever. The truth is that gender and sexual orientation are different for every person. Labels are there to help other people understand but, sometimes, it is not as simple as being just one thing. People need time to explore who they are. It felt so stressful for me to do this in such a public-facing way.

While sport as a whole was lagging behind society when it came to acceptance of difference, the beauty of it is that, ultimately, you are judged on your performance and nothing else. Even if everything was taken away from me, including all my sponsorship, any future career, whatever it was, I did not care. As long as I could still dive and be with Lance, I could be happy. I might not have any money or be liked, but I would still be a good diver. Whatever I did, there might be someone who would tell me that I was wrong, but I wanted to be strong enough to live a life that was, and always is, true to myself. To do this I knew I needed to be honest about how I felt, and that I was in a relationship with Lance, so I started to think about it and talk to my PR team, Mum and Sophie about the best way to come out. I didn't want to talk about it in a magazine or do a tell-all interview on a TV show. I didn't want anyone else twisting my words, so I decided to come out in my own way.

Every announcement I had made up to that point was via my social media channels – so I slowly started to believe that putting a short video on YouTube would be the best solution. That way I knew I could say exactly what I wanted to say and nothing more, and if anyone called up afterwards wanting any sort of clarification, I could just tell them to go back and watch the video again. I would say everything I needed to. I was also aware that I didn't want people to say I had made money out of it, so I made a point of switching off all the adverts I possibly could from this video, to de-monetise it.

One night, I sat in my bedroom and thought about exactly what I wanted to say. I needed it to be clear in my head, so I wouldn't get muddled when I spoke. I didn't want to blurt out everything, get angry or waffle, so I made some short notes and then I propped up my iPhone on my table, turned it onto selfie mode, and just started talking. Playing that video back to myself I felt physically sick and thought, 'I just can't do this, I can't put that online. There's just no way . . .'

I massively freaked out, and even having the video on my phone made me feel really anxious like it was burning a hole in my pocket. I watched it back and was surprised by the number of times that I paused and stuttered. I could tell I was incredibly nervous of getting it wrong or saying something that would offend people. Now I can see that I was just overthinking it.

I showed it to my mum, who watched it and just gave me a hug. Then I showed it to my management team too. By then they knew that it was what I wanted to do, and ultimately, it was my life. They reinforced what I already knew: I could put it out on YouTube and then it would be done, and told me: 'If this is going to make you happy Tom, you just have to do it.'

We decided together that I would film another take and put it up.

So, I did a second take in my bedroom, just me and my iPhone and all my thoughts. Then I sat on it for a few days.

I felt very, very nervous and worried. By then, I had told my brothers that Lance and I were together. Initially, they thought I was joking. Our relationship was always jokey – after my Olympic medal win, they ribbed me by saying, 'Ha ha, you came third!' It was just how we were together but quickly they cottoned on to the fact that I was being deadly serious this time. They just shrugged it off and were fine with it.

So my mum and my brothers knew the whole story, but I needed to tell the rest of my family, including my grandparents. I knew I couldn't let them find out by watching the video on YouTube, or even worse, by being told by a neighbour or someone else.

First up, I started with my dad's sister, Aunty Marie, and her husband, Uncle Jason, taking along my cousin Sam for moral support. She was absolutely great and joked with me that she had known ever since I was a toddler when I had been obsessed with having a pink tea towel wrapped around me like a skirt. Apparently, if it wasn't just perfect, correct angles and length around the ankles, I would go crazy.

My dad was always such a joker – he managed to raise a laugh in the most awkward situations and his siblings are the same. After hearing the news my dad's brother, Uncle Jamie, asked me if I wanted a cup of tea. 'How do you take it?' he asked, trying to suppress a snigger.

Aunty Marie told me what I already knew: that I had to see Grandma Rose and Grandad Dink and tell them next. I was very close to my dad's parents. They had been hugely supportive of me growing up and a massive part of my life. My parents had been together since they were just 15, and married when they were 21. I was born when Mum and Dad were 23. Grandma Rose and Grandad Dink used to live a few doors up the road from our first house in Derriford, and as a small kid I would sometimes let myself out the garden gate and toddle up to their house, with my mum having one of those moments of hideous panic thinking she had lost me until she realised where I was and found me with Grandma in the kitchen with a glass of juice. We had remained close ever since, and I know my sporting success brought them a huge sense of pride; they were often at competitions cheering me along with my dad in the crowd.

Deep down, I thought they would be fine as they loved me unconditionally, but my heart was hammering as I drove down the road and knocked on their door. As we started chatting about everyday stuff while they made us a drink, I just couldn't bear to bring it up. Eventually, I took a deep breath and summoned up the courage to speak. Originally, I had told them that the reason for Lance being in Plymouth was that he was interested in filming a documentary about me. It seemed like a good cover story.

'You know Lance, he's great, isn't he?' I started . . .

'Yes, Lance, he's a nice young man,' Grandma Rose replied.

'Well, basically, Lance and I are in a relationship,' I said.

'Of course, you are in a relationship. You're doing a documentary together,' she said.

'Er, no, not that kind of relationship. We're in a relationship with just the two of us.' I just couldn't bear to say the words, 'He's my boyfriend', or to be even more clear, 'I'm gay'.

'Of course, you are.' She wasn't quite catching on.

Then, I caught sight of Grandad in the corner, who was starting to cry. Grandad was not happy with it, and while Grandma was trying to be OK, she just wasn't.

'Come on, Tom. Do you think that is even natural?! What would your dad think?' Grandad said.

I just felt so sad that they couldn't accept it. Our relationship after that became quite strained, but going into that conversation I knew that they would either be on board with the idea or not. There was nothing that I could do to change anything. I've thought many, many times about how Dad would've felt about everything. I'm sure it might've taken him a while to get used to the idea, but above all, I know that he would want me to be happy, and I could imagine that he and Lance would've got on brilliantly. I now look back and I understand that their initial reaction came from a place of just not understanding about different sexualities, or knowing anyone else who was openly gay, but it goes without saying that I was very hurt. It also made me fear the reaction of the wider public. If my grandparents found it hard to hear, what would other people say? The fear sat heavily on my shoulders.

Then I needed to tell my other grandparents, my mum's parents. They also lived in Plymouth and I was really close to them too. I found the trip to their house unbearable. I thought my Grandma Jenny and Grandad Doug would go ballistic. Of the two sets of grandparents, I was expecting this chat to be far worse than the last one. I took them out for a meal with my mum, who knew I needed to tell them, but I couldn't bring myself to say anything.

Mum kept trying to help me by saying, 'Tom have you got something to say?' and even then I just replied, 'Yes, I wanted to thank you for coming for dinner with me.'

When Mum suggested we go back to our house for a cup of tea, I felt physically sick with nerves. My stomach was in knots, my throat was dry and hoarse, and my hands were shaking.

It was Grandad Doug who noticed my jittering hands and strange behaviour and asked if I was OK.

Mum could see I was struggling to muster up the courage, and took that as her cue to force my hand.

'Tom has something to tell you,' she said.

I just blurted out that I was releasing a video the next day. My voice was wobbling and high pitched and I didn't even pause to take a breath, it just came out in one giant sentence: 'You need to know that tomorrow I'm releasing a video online saying that I'm in a relationship with a guy it's Lance.'

'OK, but what's the big deal?' Grandma Jenny said.

'No, but Lance is my boyfriend.' I thought it was going the same way as the conversation with my Grandma Rose.

'Yes, well if you're happy, we're happy,' she said.

'That's alright,' shrugged Grandpa Doug. 'Yeah . . .'

They both gave me a hug. The relief was overwhelming and as the adrenaline started to subside, I knew that eventually, it would be fine. I had crossed the first hurdle. Now the most important people in my life knew.

The following morning was D-Day. I knew I had to just bite the bullet. I was filming for *Splash!*, where we were doing some of the 'boot camp'-style training with the celebrities in the Plymouth pool. I tried to concentrate on the job in hand but was really distracted all day, and terrified about the reaction, but after that session I only had a couple of days before I flew back to train with Jane in Houston for a few weeks. I wanted to pull the ripcord before I left in case it all went wrong, and I hoped any backlash would bypass me if I was thousands of miles away in Texas.

In a break during filming I was sitting on the floor in the corridor and didn't know what to do with myself. I had been talking with my friend Mike, who was one of the producers on the show. He was telling me it would be fine, but I was still beside myself with nerves. Andy, my coach, who was also a judge on the show, walked past. I had known him for most of my life and he had been with me through all the ups and downs. I told him what I was about to do and he gave me a big hug.

'This is a great day for you, buddy,' he said, clapping me on the back. 'It'll be fine.'

I decided to bite the bullet and just post it. With clammy hands, I clutched my phone and typed the words, 'Something I want to say . . .'

My phone blew up. I had anticipated it being a truly awful event – it was anything but. There was an outpouring of love and acceptance across social media and many friends and colleagues texted words of support. Most of all, having told the truth was a huge relief. I felt like a massive weight had been lifted from my shoulders, like I was three stone lighter than I had been before. There were a few homophobic comments on social media, but the response was overwhelmingly positive. I was so blown away by the support and encouragement. Any negativity simply didn't register. I was almost blindsided by how it had gone; never in my wildest dreams had I thought the news would be so well received. The rest of the day passed in a massive blur of filming. By the time I left the pool in Plymouth, there were already photographers gathered outside, straining their necks to try to capture me on my way out.

Off the back of the YouTube video, my management team was bombarded with interview requests from TV shows, newspapers and magazines. It felt wrong to then go to the US without saying anything publicly, and rushing off to catch a plane for a few weeks in dark glasses would defeat the object of what I had just done. I didn't feel like I should hide; I was sick of hiding. I was proud of who I was, and I no longer wanted to feel any shame.

I agreed with my manager that I would do one interview, and it was a coincidence that *The Jonathan Ross Show* was filming the night before I flew to Houston. I agreed that that would be the interview I would do. Driving around London with my mum, my cousin Sam and Sophie was utter madness. The paparazzi were all over us and at times, we couldn't even move. I had always tried to maintain a good relationship with the press and had always agreed when people asked for pictures but it had always felt quite controlled. This was on another level; there were car chases and we were followed down the streets from every angle. Photographers were madly taking pictures through car windows. It was like a game of cat and mouse. We would sneak somewhere for dinner and during dessert, the paparazzi would catch up with us. It was scary.

By then, everyone was working out who Lance was. He had been in Russia for a screening of *Milk* at a film festival, so he also had a lot going on. There was a lot of speculation about his identity and Lance confirmed it in an amusing way when he joked on Twitter: 'Slept all day today after my trip to Russia. Did I miss anything?' One of his friends quipped: 'Let me take a dive into this. Nope, everything is just swimming along,' whilst another wrote, 'No. No one's made a splash in the news world lately.'

There was some criticism of the age gap, but I had grown up fast and, in many ways, I felt older than Lance in terms of maturity. I had struggled to connect with people of my own age because of my experiences, so I think this is one of the reasons we worked and clicked. Either way, age just wasn't and never has been an issue for us. I was quickly learning that if other people had something to say or an opinion about my private life, then I would just leave them to it. Other people's opinions are not worth losing sleep over.

Sitting in front of the cameras and a live audience of the TV studio, I was in a cold sweat. Apart from talking to my friends and family, I hadn't spoken about Lance out loud to anyone, and suddenly I was on one of the UK's biggest TV shows acknowledging my sexuality and relationship. I went on just hoping to convey what I had wanted to in my video – that I was in love and happy.

'Let's deal with this: The big revelation this week. Who would've thought it, ladies and gentlemen . . . *Splash!* has a second series! What a thing, what a thing to announce!' Jonathan quipped.

The audience laughed and I stopped holding my breath, laughing with them.

'I know, I know.'

We chatted easily about the TV stuff; the ratings, the celebs who were taking part – including Jonathan's brother – and the general gossip around the show. I knew the bigger questions were coming.

'. . . which brings us to the announcement you made this week. The film you made on YouTube. Tell us about the thought process leading up to that. Why YouTube? Why now?'

I knew I could just say how I felt and approach it how I had done in every other way.

'Well to be honest, it was a terrifying decision to make,' I said. 'I didn't know what the reaction would be like, how it was going to go . . . I felt like I needed to say something. There had been rumours and speculation and I wanted to be able to say something in my own words for my heart because I didn't know what else to do. I didn't want to be caught on the back foot. I wanted to be honest and open about my life. Obviously some parts of my life are private – not very many,

I'll give you that – but I felt like I had to say something. Right now I couldn't be happier – the support has been amazing.'

I thanked everyone for their support and people cheered and someone even yelled, 'I love you Tom!' I remember I felt liberated but I think the overwhelming feeling was one of relief. I had had the courage to tell everyone on camera and now I could be myself and not worry so much.

Like the general public, the world of British diving was also fiercely protective. How my news would go down on the world sporting stage bothered me more. A year later, in 2014, I skipped a competition in Russia because I was nervous about the reaction. As well as having an injury, I was intimidated and had heard stories of beatings, kidnappings and torture of gay people. I never read too much about the exact nature of what happened but I knew it went on. Then when everyone on the diving team got back and talked about the event, I kicked myself for not going. I had made the wrong decision because I was intimidated. I told myself I would never miss another competition for that reason.

I now feel extremely lucky to be able to compete as I am, without worrying about the ramifications. I go to Russia quite often and during one competition I wore a rainbow pin badge proudly on my chest when I went to collect my medal on the podium. Far from feeling scared, it made me feel empowered. Over time my determination to be courageous had changed my mindset, and it felt important that I use my platform in a positive way. I hoped that any young Russian kids struggling with their sexuality who might've seen that would feel stronger and less oppressed. Since coming out, I've also competed in the Middle East, where being gay is a crime punishable by death in some countries. I think being able to compete and climb onto a podium as a gay man speaks louder than boycotting the event. It shows we're real and visible. It's more powerful. I hope we can get to a place in the world where people can be treated equally and judged on their performance in the field, in the pool, or wherever it is, rather than their personal life. To have an even playing field is what every sportsperson strives for and I am lucky that I am in a sport that accepts me. We have come a long way since I came out in 2013, but sometimes it is the fans more than the people within the sport that drive homophobia. I don't think people within sport care that much, but it can be upsetting when football fans, for example, use chants to demonise certain things about players – not just regarding sexuality, but also race. Overall, it is definitely changing in a positive direction and this can only be a great thing. It's only by sharing stories that we can change hearts and minds and build bridges for people who are different.

It felt good to take back control of the media narrative that surrounded me, which for a while felt out of control. It seems crazy that the video has now been watched more than twelve million times but I hope it helps other young people who might feel scared about how they feel or being different. I think that the more people talk about how they are, the more young people will feel empowered to do the same. Everyone is a little bit different in some way and it is about celebrating and embracing those differences. Those are the things that can set us apart when it comes to life experience, and by being ourselves and being authentic we can be happy.

We are often told to just be ourselves but what does that really mean? 'Just be yourself', 'just do what you want', 'just listen to your gut feelings'. There is no 'just' in any of these statements, because it is hard. I think we are often told how to be; how to behave, how to look, what to believe, and there is no part of our lives that isn't put under scrutiny in this way. We all feel the pressure to conform. Sometimes it can be really challenging to be yourself, especially when it is at odds with the mainstream. I always showed up, but for a time, I masked how I really felt and what was important to me. I felt so stifled, it was as if I had chains wrapped around me. Looking back, I wish I could've been myself unconditionally from the get-go, but I was making decisions based on fear.

I have always known who I am and what makes me happy, but acknowledging my relationship and sexuality in a wider sense made me embrace it and care less what anyone else thought about it. It seemed impossible at the time, and like I could never come out of the situation well, but now I am able to live my life authentically and be myself. I didn't want to feel ashamed, to pretend, to try to please other people, or act or be a certain way because that was society's idea of the 'right' thing to do. My focus was and is never about outward success, but more about just being honest and living with integrity. We should all be free to explore who we are and not worry about what is 'right' or 'wrong'. I was wracked with doubts but I knew I wanted to live my life on my terms and by my rules. I am far happier for it.

ACCEPTANCE

People lose people in many different ways. Slowly, quickly, unexpectedly. Everyone deals with it differently and manages grief in the best way they can. Each experience is unique. I have learned since losing my dad in 2011, that there is no finish line when it comes to grieving and I have learned to sit more comfortably with my feelings. I have realised that trying to suppress my emotions simply made them seep into other parts of my life, stopping me from being fully present in the best moments. I didn't grieve the loss of my dad properly for a long time, and whilst I will never be the same person I was when he was here, I am able to talk about him and keep the memory of him alive. I have learned the ability to grieve and accept my feelings.

Dad poured his love and time into family life, making pancakes for breakfast, helping me and my brothers learn to walk, run and read, making us laugh until we cried as we bundled onto him on the sofa; he was always by our sides.

I started diving when I was 7. We lived by the sea in Plymouth and like all parents, mine wanted me to be a good swimmer and be able to handle myself in the water. There were diving classes being advertised at the local pool and I was instantly captivated by the older children hurling themselves off the boards at all angles. My dad said William and I could have a go and shelled out £25 in crisp notes for five lessons. For a while, William was better than me and picked up the dives far quicker. There was a real sense of fun competition between us. After a while, he became more interested in other sports and gave up but I continued with weekly classes. It had piqued my interest and my parents were happy because I had found something I was interested in and enjoyed. I started to work my way through the different certificates and before long, I could perform tricky dives that no one else in my group could. One weekly session became two and then I was competing in the squad team and winning trophies. Before long, I was training more, spending hours every week preparing my body for events and going away on camps. I travelled to Australia on my own with the team at the age of 10.

When I went away to diving training camp when I was

young, I was so homesick. I suffered from awful insomnia and would call my parents crying late at night, threatening to throw myself out the window and say I would rather be dead than at whatever camp it was. I obviously didn't mean any of it but just felt my emotions really strongly and wasn't afraid to voice them.

My parents were a driving force in making me feel safe. When they could, my mum and dad would come to the camps, rock up at the next-door hotel and remain there for the duration, reminding me during my nightly outbursts they were nearby. I loved the days when I was diving with my friends and would forget the fuss of the evening before; the pangs of homesickness would only appear at night times when I was trying to sleep. Instead of telling me to feel a certain way, that I was being silly, or to go to bed and stop being a baby, Mum and Dad would always try to empathise with me and ask me questions to help me work out why I felt a certain way. By the time I had talked it out, I would understand more about why I was feeling upset or sad. I would then go to sleep and wake up the next day, raring to go for another day of diving. I struggled with feeling like this for years and was homesick every time I went away until I was around 13 when I grew out of it. Every time, almost without fail, we would go through the same dramas, but my parents never dismissed my feelings.

Unlike many parents who have children who are into sport,

and who try to get themselves up on the technical detail, so they can try to 'improve' their children and give them pointers by the poolside, my parents never attempted to do this. They never even tried to understand it. Dad always came with me wherever I went – we called him 'taxi driver dad' as he ferried me three miles from our home to training at the Mayflower Centre multiple times a week, and then to competitions around the country. But he never tried to see things that I needed to improve or work on. He never told me my attitude was wrong, that I wasn't training hard enough, what I should eat, or commented on how much I slept; he never tried to do that. He was just there for me. He would sit in the balcony and watch. If we were at a competition, I would look out for his giant Union Jack flag and he was always, always waving it from the stands. We had spent a lot of our childhood holidays in our caravan, travelling to Cornwall or France, and the flag was originally a giant beach towel that was big enough for the whole family to sit on. He worked so, so hard and would always be at every competition, even in some of the most far-flung places around the world. When they could, my whole family would come too. As far as Dad was concerned, every dive I did was a good one. In 2009 in Rome, after I had become the youngest-ever British World Champion in any sport at the age of 15, I had been whisked straight into a room for the press conference. As I sat at the table at the front of the room, someone at the back put their hand up, as if they wanted to ask a question. It was Dad and I could see everyone looking confused: Who was this guy?

'I'm Tom's dad. Come and give me a cuddle,' he said. I was slightly embarrassed but he did not care what the world thought of the slightly overweight middle-aged man sobbing with pride. He loved my competitions and was my biggest cheerleader. Outside of diving, Dad was fun – he was always laughing and joking, he was always making other people smile and brought joy, and chocolate, wherever he went. He loved with his entire heart and would always go out of his way for anyone, particularly our family.

Dad was first diagnosed with a brain tumour in 2006. For a long time, I did not understand what it meant or what cancer really was. For some time before his diagnosis, he had been having strange episodes where he said he felt like his head was filling up with water like he was hallucinating. One day he scraped the car when he was driving to work and wasn't sure what was happening. He had gone backwards and forwards from the GP, who put it down to stress and even sent him to a psychiatrist because he was convinced it was not a physical issue. Dad had a busy home and work life and was only in his mid-thirties. I had no idea how serious it was; now I know that when he eventually received the diagnosis, the tumour was the size of a grapefruit. I was just a kid and when we arrived at the hospital after an operation to cut most of the tumour out, he had bandages all around his head. Dad told me that he had been given a fiver by everyone at the local pub to shave his head for Comic Relief. Initially, I was never aware that he was so ill because I never saw my mum or my grandma crying.

We danced and laughed our way through the annual 'Rob's still here' party at the local pub, with his cancer controlled with treatment and medication. He had an incredible sense of humour and always saw the bright side of any situation, even cancer. I never once saw him complain, moan or be upset. When he went into the MRI scanner for regular scans he complained that he looked like Homer Simpson. When anyone asked him how he felt, full of concern, he always said, 'About nineteen.'

He had the words printed on a T-shirt, 'Give me oil in my lamp, keep me burning.' To me, he was infallible.

When his cancer came back five years after the initial diagnosis, I was aware that this was not good news, but that I needed to be strong for my mum and my two brothers; William is two years younger and Ben is five years younger than me. Diving became even more of a focus. Dad was my greatest champion of all, and as he became more unwell, he started to plan his time around my competitions and increasing numbers of hospital appointments. Soon, he was unable to come to international competitions, after doctors warned that it wasn't safe for him, so he stayed home when I competed in the Commonwealth Games in Delhi in 2010. It was the first big competition I had taken part in that he hadn't been on the balcony, waving his giant flag. As always, I packed my lucky monkey – a cuddly toy that my parents had bought for me and that had travelled with me since I was a child suffering from awful homesickness. It was a brilliant competition and I won a gold on the ten-metre synchro with my partner Max Brick and then a day later I clinched the gold in the individual event. I called Dad immediately from the poolside and he told me he had been glued to the television.

'You did it, Tom!' he cried. He was thrilled.

Slowly Dad seemed to get worse but we didn't dwell on it. We made small changes like giving him his tea in his right hand, rather than his left, and he just got with life with as little fuss as possible, ploughing on. Both my dad and my mum shielded me from the harsh reality of what was happening.

In his final days, when his health was deteriorating more quickly, the question of me stopping diving was never an option. I got up in the morning, went to school, to training, to competitions, and there was no way that my continued participation in any of these was up for debate. I always held on to the hope that he would bounce back from his illness, as he had done before.

I was called back from a training camp in Guadalajara in Mexico in April 2011 and at first, I didn't understand the enormity of this and couldn't really comprehend what my mum was saying – I was expecting to travel with the team for a competition to Fort Lauderdale in Florida a few days later. I never thought Dad was going to die; he had made light of his illness for so many years and had always picked himself back up after setbacks. It was a particularly hard conversation and my mum had to tell me that he did not have long left – he might only last hours, a day, a week, maybe. I immediately packed my bags and started the agonizingly slow journey home. The minutes crept by as I sat restless in my seat with a million thoughts whirring around my head.

When Dad saw me back in our family home by his bedside, he raised an arm slowly and punched the air, as if to say, 'March on, Tom's home!' The whole family was there – my grandparents and aunts and uncles. I had to tell Ben that Dad was going to die; I just don't think that my mum could find the words. I'm not sure how I managed.

Some days, Dad was lucid and asking about whether his front row tickets for 2012 had arrived, and testing me on my driving theory because I was starting to learn to drive. He had struggled to try to get out of his metal hospital bed, which we had set up in the front room, to watch me crawl down the road at ten miles per hour on my first driving lesson, having just turned 17. He had lost sight in his left eye by then, so I sat and talked by his right side and syringed water into his mouth. On other days, he slept and his breathing was laboured as the family sat around, not knowing what to say or whether to sleep. I felt completely out of my depth. The only thing that raised a smile was the diving team, who put my face on wooden spoons and sent me pictures of 'me' on the end of the board, pretending I was still with them.

Incredibly, Dad made it through my seventeenth birthday, then Ben's twelfth birthday a couple of weeks later, missing William's fifteenth birthday by three days. He was a real fighter and he had consistently challenged all predictions from his doctors of what might happen or how long he had left. I never lost hope that he might pull through.

He passed away on 27 May 2011, aged just 40, with all of us holding his hands.

After he died, I went straight back into training, not missing a single session. I had tunnel vision and didn't want to think about it. It was like I had blinkers on. At his funeral, I left the wake early to travel to Leeds for the National Championships. I didn't perform that well, 'duffing' a couple of dives, as Dad would say, and coming second to Pete Waterfield. Now it seems crazy that I competed, but I had become used to compartmentalising my life and putting my feelings into a box. I had found it easy to divide the different parts of my life – my family life, school life, diving and any media work – into separate spaces, and I was determined to keep trying to do that. I would keep everything safely zipped in its separate box. As I had become busier at school and started travelling around the world, I had found this system effective for managing my time and, to a certain extent, my emotions. It had worked for me before then. I felt like I should be there, back at the poolside, for Dad, and that I would be letting him down in some way if I wasn't. I knew it was where he would want me to be.

When people tried to speak to me about Dad, I did my best to be honest but I felt so many different and complex emotions that I almost couldn't process the enormity of losing him. When I passed my driving test a few weeks after he passed away, I picked up the phone and dialled his number automatically before realising my mistake with a sudden rush of anger and upset, and hanging up. I kept expecting him to walk through the door with a practical joke. And thinking about how he spoke, the exact pressure of his arms when he hugged me. It just didn't seem real. I also felt an immense responsibility to help my mum to make sure my brothers were OK and that we had enough money to survive, and by then my sponsorship deals were providing good financial stability. I never really talked about Dad, especially with my brothers. We joked about him to try to capture some of his humour, but he had left a void and an immense spirit that was impossible to replace.

A few weeks after the funeral, with the prospect of the run-up to London 2012 just months away, the rounds of interviews started and inevitably people asked me about Dad. Despite my management trying to protect me and divert questions with firm shakes of the head and clear instructions to leave me alone and not ask those questions, journalists persisted in asking how I was feeling.

How was I feeling? Raw, numb, heartbroken. I felt everything and nothing. I had not even started to process what had happened. I would say the same line about how he wanted me to continue diving. That was one thing I knew, and that I could hold onto. Travelling with the team provided a space where I could forget and allowed my brain to concentrate on something else. At home, there was an overwhelming sadness shrouding the house and everyone there, and diving felt like a sort of escape. I think it probably brought a sense of comfort to the family too; Dad was so focused on it, so it became a linchpin for the family. The knowledge that my diving meant so much to him too propelled us all through the long days that followed his death. The day after the funeral, my mum and brothers were also watching the National Championships on the balcony in Leeds. The giant Union Jack flag was conspicuous in its absence.

I had been quite involved with the press around the Olympics as one of the *Daily Mail*'s 'Magnificent 7', a group of seven Olympic hopefuls that they had picked out and been following for the seven years in the run-up to the competition. As part of that and, along with other press to publicise the Olympics, we had toured around the London Aquatics Centre designed by the incredible British-Iraqi architect Zaha Hadid, as it grew from the ground upwards, taking on its recognisable unique shape. I had posed with my hard hat on the diving boards, which felt amazing and so unlike the diving boards I knew; they were like waves coming out of the floor.

My dad's ashes were placed into gold hearts for my mum, my brothers and I to treasure forever. But the majority of his ashes now sit underneath the floor of the steps of the diving board at this London centre. By the time that the competitions started taking place at the start of 2012, they had dug up a chunk of floor and put him down there in a box. It meant that he could be there in some way. His ashes sit underneath a metal disc and that is where I always put my water bottle when I am training. I knew that I would never be able to tell him how my diving was going in person but this knowledge brought with it some comfort. Dad would know how I was getting on. I would be able to picture his face and remember his words of encouragement.

In the run-up to 2012, every day's training was carefully mapped out. There was a solid structure that brought routine and the sense of purpose was colossal. Every small effort was recognised as we moved forwards to the ultimate goal. I felt like I had trained for that competition most of my conscious life.

Parents and family members were not allowed on the pool – side and struggled to get tickets at all for my events in 2012

– in the end my mum had to threaten to not sign the waiver for me to compete. So my dad, in his position beneath the diving board steps, had the best seat in the house.

My dad not physically being there in London 2012 and in the immediate aftermath felt raw. I touched the part of the step where he was before I went up to perform each dive. I was quite superstitious then and it felt important that I did that. Then suddenly, it had happened: I had a bronze medal around my neck and looked into the audience – Mum was there, my brothers, and everyone was jumping around and cheering in delight. No Dad. I couldn't see the big flag he always took with him. I remembered looking up into the rafters and seeing all the flags of the participating nations and the Union Jack flag being the biggest one, and thinking 'Holy crap, Dad, we did it.' I knew he would've wanted to bundle himself into the pool with the diving team in that moment of celebration and would be bobbing about right in the middle, his bald head shining out with the best of them.

I thought of it as 'our' success and that 'we' had won a medal. It was never just 'I' or 'me'; it felt like a big team effort. This included the wider team like Andy and my diving mates, but was more about Dad and I, as if he had never passed away. His hugs and the feeling of his arms around me still felt very real. But not being able to witness his joy in that moment felt awful. I wasn't sure how I was supposed to feel; whether I was supposed to sit around and cry. I tried to brush away my feelings as best I could and enjoy the moment.

When Lance moved to London he noticed that I was not very openly affectionate. I was nervous to get close to him.

One day, we were at Westfield in Stratford and coming down the escalator. Lance went to put his arm around me and I immediately tensed up.

'Why do you do that?' he asked.

I knew what he meant.

'You can be open with me,' he said. 'Let my love in – don't push it away.'

We started to talk about how I was feeling and why I was not very tactile.

'I know,' I sighed. 'I am just so paranoid about losing people. I am worried that something will take you away from me.'

'Listen, I am not going to disappear or vanish. I love you.'

No one had ever openly confronted me about my inability to allow people in before; it was like my emotions surrounding my dad's death had been swept under a rug, never to be upturned in the fear we would all just fall apart. I think no one else wanted to talk to me about him because they didn't want to upset me. On the occasions where I felt able to talk about him, I never wanted to talk to those closest to me because I did not want to upset them or make them feel awkward either. I also felt like I had to be the man of the house, and the one to look after everyone else, which made it hard for me to open up with my family. I needed to be strong for them.

But Lance having brought this up with me opened up a new conversation, and we sat down over lunch and talked more about why I was so closed off. I knew if I opened my heart up, it was susceptible to breaking. I wasn't afraid of Lance breaking up with me – I felt 100 per cent secure in our relationship – but of me losing him in a way that I couldn't control. We talked about how the fear stemmed from me losing my dad and the fact that I had not really processed it. I came to realise that I couldn't close off my heart for my whole life, and that it was only by dealing with my grief that I would be able to feel the depth of emotions.

'You need to start speaking to someone,' Lance said. 'Or speak to me. I want to know how you are feeling. Talk to me about how you feel about your dad.'

It wasn't until this conversation that I realised just how emotionally shut-off I was. I would never reflect and would just always go, go, go and put on a brave face regardless of how I felt. Lance told me that I needed to be vulnerable around him and let down my guard. If I was having a bad day, I would have to tell him and talk about it and sit with my grief, rather than pushing it away. Only then could he support me through it. If I couldn't count on him, who could I count on? Until then, I hadn't even tried to understand my emotions. It was only when I sat down with myself to really process what I had been through that I was able to soak in both the good and the bad.

Slowly I started to think and talk about the things I missed about my dad, even as simple as him cooking a stir-fry for us on a Friday night or ordering a Chinese takeaway on a Saturday.

'Why have you stopped doing that?' Lance asked, one evening after I had mentioned how I missed it.

'It just reminds me of Dad too much.'

'Let's keep those traditions going and celebrate them and keep that memory going because that's what you did with him.'

'Now you talk about it like that, it makes more sense.'

Grief does not fit neatly into five stages and nor should I feel the pressure to 'move on' and ever leave him behind. Dad will always be part of me; it's not like the emotions I feel will ever magically disappear – I just have to sit with them and not try to avoid or fix them.

Now, when I have a good training session or a successful competition, I often think, 'I wonder what Dad would think of this?' I regularly reflect on what kind of grandad he would be and find myself smiling. He behaved like a big kid himself a lot of the time, so I know he would've been in his element. I know I'll never know the answers, and that's hard, but I am learning to live more comfortably with my memories of him. I learned through time and trust that it was OK to have a bad day and talk about how I miss him. It's not always perfect; on joyous occasions such as my wedding and Robbie's birth, I felt a slight disassociation, like I was sitting through some sort of TV show of my life. I felt as if Dad should've been there on the front row at my wedding cracking jokes, or cuddling his first grandson by my mum's side. It was as if my brain protected me against the worst emotions but also the best ones. But I have got better at recognising moments where I miss him, and now I can share those thoughts and stories from when he was alive. I want to remember those particularly special times.

I now realise that emotional health is not only feeling positive emotions but feeling a full spectrum of emotions, and that talking about my innermost feelings, however sad, bad or ugly, is not a sign of weakness – it's a sign of strength. Initially, it was very scary to talk about how I felt, but as I opened up it made more sense. Now I have a much more open dialogue with both my family and with Lance. We talk about Dad, keep his memory alive with stories from the past, and I talk about how I feel. I accept the ups and downs and the rockiness of the journey. It is a much healthier and happier way to be. Tuning in to those emotions and accepting them allows me to figure out what I need in the moment. Through acceptance, I now have a deeper sense of being and peace.

PURPOSE

In the run-up to the London 2012 Olympics, my schedule had been so rigid, and for a long time before then I had been balancing my school work with my training. After the bullying episodes at my first secondary school, I was offered a scholarship at Plymouth College. At the time, the decision to leave my friends felt hard but the environment was completely different and I quickly made new friends with a group of competitive swimmers.

As the schoolwork ramped up, I was also spending up to six hours in the pool every day. I split my A levels across three years, allowing me to ease off studying in the run-up to the Olympics. I would go to school for the first two lessons, then go to training for two and a half hours, then head back to school for lunch and two more lessons. I would then train for another two and a half hours, before having dinner, doing my homework and going to bed.

As the days passed after the 2012 Olympics, I no longer had to stick to the same regimented and hectic routine that I had before, and my ninety-five miles per hour ride came to a screeching halt. As liberating as this was in one sense, I also felt slightly adrift. I couldn't vocalise this at all, despite the fact I was always surrounded by my friends. I had been taught that I could push through anything and I had shown that I could; I had made it to where I wanted to be, so it didn't even occur to me to talk to anyone about how I felt. I knew it would be impossible for anyone to understand unless they were walking in my shoes because it did not really make sense, even to me.

The attributes that make up a successful sportsperson are like an intricate jigsaw, but commitment, ambition and focus all rank really highly. Any athlete can tell you that after the Olympics, with no other competition of that magnitude on the horizon, it can feel impossible to muster the same levels of focus and drive. In any sporting event, competitors can be physically on a par with each other, but what is going on in our minds is what sets us apart. The mental game. And the post-Olympics blues are real. For me, at just 18 years old, and having always been labelled as 'just' a diver, the months following the 2012 Olympics made me question whether diving was really what I wanted to do. I'd just achieved the win that

I'd been working for all of my life; there were countless opportunities and I felt that I needed to explore them in order to know what I wanted. It was a period in my life when I needed to find out more about myself and what mattered most to me.

So it's no surprise that, shortly after the Olympics, I started to struggle to focus on my sport. I had bought my first home in Plymouth, not far from my family house. It was a five-bedroom house with a big garden and I always had friends with me. I was partying a lot and every weekend everyone would come back to mine, bundling into the living room. It was your typical young person's house with empty beer bottles and pizza boxes stacked on every surface, sleeping bags on the floor, and dirty washing piled high; I look back now and wonder how I survived amongst the chaos. I had also bargained with my coach, Andy, that I wouldn't dive on weekends. Before then, I had only had a Sunday off. Now it seemed important to me that I could skip Saturday's session so I could enjoy both Friday and Saturday nights going out in town, drinking and partying with my friends. My resolve to keep working as hard as I could was wavering, and I definitely wasn't helping myself.

I had always done various media and partnerships work but, post-Olympics, the branding and media offers coming my way ramped up and it was hard to know which way I could or should turn. With every new opportunity to work with someone new, with a different fee attached, came a decision, and there were at least five different pathways mapped out into the future. It was like one of those children's gamebooks, where if you choose one journey you end up skipping all of the other narratives – I wanted desperately to explore all of them. I was struggling with my Twister and, for a time, I felt strongly that I wanted to give up diving. But the bigger question was what I would do next. Diving was all I had ever wanted to do. If I didn't want to dive anymore, what would I be?

I wondered about all sorts of stuff: whether I could be an actor, a singer, a TV host, I mean . . . why not? I was pretty naïve and was looking for any route out of being a diver. The prospect of more competitions, and Rio 2016, just didn't register on my radar. Four years is a long, long time for an 18-year-old. I wanted something else to come round that would be so different, so exciting, so captivating, that I didn't have to think and worry about diving. It was like I was having a mid-life crisis at the age of 18; I was a kid, crazily trying to clamber his way blindly out of a black hole. Now I see that I was just running away because I was unhappy in myself.

I'd always loved the television work that I had done. I had starred in a couple of documentaries about my life, been on some quiz shows as a celebrity panellist, and starred in TV fundraisers like *Sport Relief,* a Comic Relief charity event. I loved interacting with new people, and doing this live on TV brought with it a real rush of adrenaline. So, I leaped at two opportunities that materialised in 2013 with the television production company TwoFour, who wanted me to act as an expert mentor to celebrities learning to dive in a programme called *Splash!*, as well as to present a travelogue series where I'd be backpacking around the world.

The whole idea of *Splash!* seemed crazy; if someone had told me ten years prior that there was going to be a prime-time Saturday night TV show about diving, with a bunch of celebrities in Lycra and lipstick, I would never have believed them. Let alone me being at the heart of it in my trunks. It was also very specialist, and needed professional divers to train and judge the contestants. They couldn't just draft anyone in, which meant that lots of people were working on the show that I knew. Andy was one of the judges, along with former Olympic silver medallist Leon Taylor, who had been a bit of a mentor to me in my younger diving days, and comedian Jo Brand. All of my diving community was there in some shape or form, so it was like having the best parts of my sport, combined with a whole new dimension of entertainment and TV. Being a new format also made it exciting: bright lights throughout the Olympic-sized pool in Luton meant it could be lit like a TV studio, cameramen navigated the high boards and were in the pool, treading water in wetsuits.

All the stars trained with diving instructors at pools closer to where they were living and working, but they would travel down each week to Plymouth where I was running 'boot camp'-style training camps. I would train in the morning, complete a couple of hours of *Splash!* filming, and then I would come back to my own training and diving in the afternoon.

It was interesting getting to meet the celebrities, and for me to see how the psychology I took for granted was being challenged by people I had seen on the TV or knew from elsewhere. Whatever their physical diving ability, they were all really, really scared. There were a few occasions when contestants would jump off the board, thinking they were invincible, that it would be easy, or that they could basically fly. They would have a moment of clarity before their brain and self-preservation instinct would kick in and they would decide that they didn't want to be there. There was a lot of arm flapping, swearing and bruises.

The whole issue of pushing the contestants to higher boards quite quickly for the show was a learning curve for everyone. When one of the stars could complete a good dive from three metres, we would then send them up to do it off five metres. Even though the dive would be exactly the same with a millisecond longer in the air, I could see how much it changed the way they thought about it and how that impacted what their bodies did in the air and then how they landed. One of my tricks with the contestants on *Splash!* was that if they were scared to go off the five-metre board, I would take them up to the ten-metre board and spend a bit of time up there until they were all terrified, before bringing them back down to five metres. Then it wouldn't feel as high or scary, so they would be able to do the dive. I had experienced celebs not wanting to dive off the high board before: a few years earlier, I had done a sketch with James Corden as Smithy for *Sport Relief*, and it had taken three and a half hours to coax him off the end.

Talent shows like *Strictly Come Dancing* and *Dancing On Ice* involve an element of dressing up and flamboyant costumes; in *Splash!* all the celebs had to strip down to their swimming shorts or costumes, which was a great leveller as there was only so much dressing up any of them could do. The costumes were hilarious, but they were only ever going to be swimwear that covered so much. I had loads of honest conversations about how they found the idea of standing up on a board wearing so few clothes almost as stressful as the diving itself. They found the diving scary, but having to be confident in their own skin was another challenge that they hadn't imagined would be an issue when they were standing at the end of the diving board.

In the end, we filmed two seasons of *Splash!*, but after that my schedule meant that I couldn't feasibly tie myself up for a third, so the show was shelved. As it was, there were people in the diving world already telling me that my TV work was a diversion from my sport. The then CEO of British Swimming, David Sparkes, spoke out to the press about how it was 'putting the horse before the cart' when it came to my career, and how the Chinese divers didn't have TV shows distracting them. He said publicly that I needed to work harder. He might have had a point, but he made it badly; he never directly spoke to me about his concerns and it felt really underhand to be criticised so brutally via the press. I felt like he was attacking me, an 18-year-old, for doing something different, even though it wasn't interfering with my training schedule. The fact that my dad had recently passed away, and that I felt as though I was responsible for supporting my family through work in this way, was not considered before he spoke to the press. My experiences as an individual, and any mental health issues that I could have suffered because of these, consequently didn't feel as though they were a priority. No one ever asked me what my motivation was for the work I'd been doing; if David had spoken to me directly, he might have understood a small amount of what I was going through and why I had made the decision to be on TV. It was pretty disrespectful, to say the least.

In the end, my mum played him at his own game and wrote an open letter to him, explaining how hard I had worked, post-Olympics, how I had struggled with the loss of my dad and to stay motivated, and how I had promoted UK sport, amongst other things. She also highlighted something that not a lot of people realise – that I was funding all my own diving. I don't get paid to dive. The powers that be might've had an opinion about what I did away from the diving pool, even though it didn't eat into any of my training time, but they had also taken away my salary. As soon as you take on a certain level of sponsorship, you lose funding, so the only way I could earn money to support myself, and my sport, was through sponsorship and other work. I didn't have a choice. When it came to the watchful eyes of British Swimming, it felt like the more successful I became, the more I should be punished. I never wanted to read any newspaper articles or get involved. My mum wanted to stick up for her son and I couldn't stop her; it felt good that we had a voice. I think it was received well publicly, and David Sparkes always dealt with things better from then on until he retired in 2017. I tried to shut myself off from it a bit, because it felt like everyone had an opinion when I was simply trying to forge a future and find a path that was right for me.

In between the two series of *Splash!* I went travelling for six weeks with Sophie for the ITV2 show, *Tom Daley Goes Global*. We went on an epic journey to Thailand, Japan, New Zealand, Australia, Spain, France, Switzerland and Morocco, staying in different places every night, from a beachside hut in Thailand which had wall-to-wall spiders, to a pod hotel in Japan, which was basically a box with no bed.

Packing for our trip, like a typical backpacker I wondered how many pairs of pants I should take with me, or whether my sleeping bag would be warm enough. Travelling on the show was fantastic. We went to so many fantastic places and at the end of each leg of our travels, I did some kind of adrenalin-fuelled extreme sport, like bungee jumping, skydiving, flying a fighter jet, and paragliding to raise money for The Brain Tumour Charity.

Guilt about taking time off training was never far away, but I rationalised in my head that the time away was a bit like a gap year, condensed into six weeks. I'd felt like I had missed out on so much up until that point, because I had been an athlete my whole life. I was always given two weeks off every year, and we had spent them on family holidays. I was well travelled, in the sense that I had travelled so much with the diving team, but it was very regimented. We would only see the coach, hotel and pool, and maybe the odd tourist attraction if there were a few hours free. But this trip was just for me (and Sophie, of course!) and looking back, I now see how much I needed it. Going to places where there were no diving boards made me happy, and I avoided swimming pools.

The trip was a very eye-opening experience, and the perfect way to blow off some steam and allow me to be away from diving, and to evaluate what I wanted and needed in my life going forwards. Having that time and freedom gave me space away from Plymouth, diving and my family, so I could re-set and start to think about the possibilities for my future. I started to properly consider my options; I thought about moving to America and training at one of the colleges there, and was thinking more and more about moving to London and training from the Olympic pool. I had met Lance by this stage and he had made me want to push myself again and be the best I could be. It made me re-focus on what I really wanted. I did not want to be at home waiting for him to call; his drive to be at the top of his game rubbed off on me, and I also felt the desire to try to find a way back to the top of my game.

Some of the high points around that trip were the sporting challenges. I am a real adrenalin seeker. Outside of diving, I love horror movies – a night in with *American Psycho* or *The Shining* is a night well spent as far as I am concerned. I will always seek out the highest and scariest rollercoaster ride at any theme park, and go on it a few times for good measure. Even completing a world-famous bungee jump off the Verzasca Dam in the Swiss Alps didn't give me that much of a rush. One of the sports involved hurling myself of a 350-foot cliff in New Zealand on a canyon swing – it was ten times the height of the diving board I was used to leaping off – and doing as many somersaults as I could before I reached the end. I successfully beat the previous record of ten held by a Swedish gymnast, managing twelve, and that was a real buzz.

I had always wanted to do a skydive. It was one of my lifelong goals, but before that trip I could never get insurance and I was never allowed. Now was the time. It was during the first leg of the trip in Thailand. On the morning of the skydive there was some awful weather with thunderstorms.

We flew up in a small plane above the clouds and weather and were trying to find a spot between the thunderstorms to jump through. It seemed quite extreme! Now I am older, I wonder why I did those things, as I'm not sure I would be quite so carefree now, but back then, I felt quite reckless. I hadn't been allowed to do anything like that because of my diving but, for once, I just didn't care. It was the first time I had put myself first, and had felt like an independent adult, where I could do what I wanted, when I wanted. As I felt the rush of freefalling through the air, and the wind blasting against my face, pushing against my cheeks, it was an incredible sensation of speed and freedom.

Immediately after the show wrapped, I went to stay with Lance in LA for two weeks and I started feeling a renewed sense of purpose as I planned my future. Having spent some time away, diving no longer seemed at the centre of everything; my world now seemed much bigger. I decided that although being just 'comfortable' was fine I wanted more than that. I wanted to start pushing myself again, and I had more ambition and drive to make changes that would work for me and for Lance.

I enjoyed getting back to the pool and back to training. I felt like I had blown off the steam that I needed to. Some days, the distance between me and Lance felt so big. We were both busy; Lance with his film career and me with my training. For some time I had wondered whether I needed a move to London to change things up. It would allow me to attend the odd party or event when it didn't interfere with my training. One of the biggest reasons to move was the fact that it would make it easier for our relationship. Los Angeles to London was long-distance enough, but Plymouth to LA was even bigger. There was a fantastic new diving pool in Plymouth at the Plymouth Life Centre, that had become my new training home after it opened in March 2012, but equally, at the London Aquatics Centre there was a state-of-the-art pool, gym and dry area, all of which I needed to train. In Plymouth, I felt there was an expectation and focus on me that just wasn't there when I was in London. After meeting Lance, we decided that moving there would work for us as a couple. He had sacrificed so much for me to live near a ten-metre board, and being in London made more sense for him than settling in Plymouth. With his support, I really started to believe that if I could dream it, I could do it.

After we got together, I no longer feared taking risks or making changes. Yes, I was comfortable in Plymouth, but comfort doesn't make you the best at what you do.

The move felt like a leap of faith but I could see it would also lead to other opportunities. There were discussions about opening a diving academy in my name if I started training at the London Aquatic Centre, and I felt passionate about getting as many young kids into the sport that I loved as possible. There are now Tom Daley Diving Academies at pools all over the country.

By then, the decision had been made that I would train with Jane and she would also make the move to London. We came together at the right time for both of us, and her presence felt like an injection of something new and fresh into my training. Andy had been technically great; he had taught me every single dive from scratch and everything I knew.

Jane brought something different to the table. She had seen me in competitions and observed many of my performances. She told me about the things she would like to 'fix' about my diving. We started talking about all the 'one per cents' outside of the pool that might work towards my success and optimise my performance, like nutrition, recovery, and other parts of my training that could feed towards being a professional athlete. Those tiny incremental changes that could help me. We had been doing our best in Plymouth, and doing what we thought was right, but Jane had been coaching in the American college system for a number of years, where they have the most high-tech science equipment and expertise to support your sport. There were so many people studying who wanted to help and support me, so it was a really eye-opening experience. During my first trip out to Houston, we had spoken to one of the nutritionists and I learned a lot very, very quickly about what and how I should be eating. British sport and British diving were never set up in quite the same way to give athletes that level of expertise.

Jane and I motivated each other. She was always so positive

and happy during our sessions, and she had and still has a killer desire to win. She wants to win and will do anything to get you there. I respected that drive and it helped to re-ignite my passion to be the best in every competition I could.

My training took on a new tack – it was more structured and focused than it had been, and with the innovation of my new Firework dive, and renewed sense of motivation and focus, my diving started to take a front seat again. Some days things felt a little bit scary and daunting but that also felt exciting. Now I had been given the opportunity to explore different things, I knew that diving was what I loved. We agreed that I would still do other work because I wanted and needed to. Jane was clear about the time she needed to train with me and everything else then slotted around that.

Any relationship between an athlete and coach is complex and unique. Jane and I went through a real honeymoon phase as we got to know each other, but after that had faded, we needed to work out our boundaries and that was much harder. We often butted heads about what I was doing away from the pool and my personal life. Having a coach when you're a professional athlete can be like being parented again; as an adult, no one really wants that. As my life expanded beyond diving, there was a constant push and pull of commitment between sport and my family life.

For six months, it was just Jane and I training at the pool, and this also brought with it its own challenges because it was very intense. The spotlight was firmly fixed on me and there was no opportunity to take a rest. We started to look for other divers and soon we had a small team of elite divers, so we could be a complete team, and Jane was helping take their careers to the next level. Now, the diving academy in London is thriving, and on the elite side of the club, most of the Olympic platform hopefuls train in London together.

As I settled into my new training regime, Lance and I found our first place together and moved in. He was still spending a lot of time in LA for work, but would also be with me when he could. We enjoyed making our home together and learning more about each other. I had gone from feeling despondent to becoming more motivated to have my own success and to not be hanging around at home waiting for him. We found that our outlooks on life and the way we structured our days were so different but also they also started to complement each other. I tend to like to have every aspect of my day including my spare time drilled down to the last minute, even on my days off, whereas Lance takes a more relaxed and spontaneous approach to life. Our relationship taught me to slow down and let go of things that I couldn't control. We spent our free time doing what every other couple does: going for brunches, seeing friends, and learning more about each other.

After this time, I started to see my fate mapped out more clearly. I knew that maybe in the future I could try to transfer all my passion and work ethic to a new career, but while I could still compete, I knew diving was still what I wanted to do. It was a gift and I wanted to enjoy it for as long as I could. I still had that fire in my belly to win and be the best at what I did.

There was also a freedom that came with coming out to the world, moving to London and living in a way that I wanted, and that suited Lance and me. It was liberating.

*   *   *

Labels are for clothes. They take on an 'all or nothing' meaning. It is so easy to put yourself in a box. As soon as I stepped away from the diving board and took a break, I realised I was more than just a diver: I was a gay man, a friend, a son, a brother, and a person who loved media work, cheesecake, exercise and travelling the world. Doing other things kept my mind fresh. It is so easy to be trapped. A sexual identity, a job, a status; I could see that I could be more than that. I could do better and be better.

I took ownership of my own life; what I needed and wanted and how I saw my future. I started to see a life that was not just about diving objectives and winning medals and being an Olympian. I began to see my results through a lens of these things not being solely what defined me. Diving was something I could do but it wasn't who I was. This realisation brought with it a profound sense of freedom and release. I started to find myself enjoying each moment in the pool. I could be a diver when I was at the pool, and have a life outside of that. I started to make the 'job'; it didn't make me.

ENDURANCE

Standing at the back of the board in one of the huge stadiums in Beijing for the FINA World Series competition in March 2018, I made my normal mental preparations for my front four and a half somersaults dive, envisaging the precise and swift motions in my head. It's a crucial dive in my set because it has the highest level of difficulty. When I originally learned this dive, before London 2012, it was dubbed 'the most difficult dive in the world' because it takes just over a second to complete and the finish is low, with none of what we call 'float time' in the air before hitting the water. Usually, though, this dive came naturally to me. I just had to run up to the end of the platform, throw myself off, get into a tight tuck shape, hold on, and then line up towards the water when I got there. Andy used to call it a 'chorine sniffer': a dive where you get as close to the water as you can, close enough to smell it, before kicking out fast. It's not like my twisting dive, where I have to think carefully about the multiple sections of the dive. I had been having particular trouble with this dive that season, and on that day, I was really struggling with it and I was nervous. I was in constant agony with my hips and shins. Whenever everything ached, throbbed or was tender in previous years, I was still able to make all my dives. This felt completely different. I had stopped being able to actually make this specific dive at all.

I had been suffering from problems in my hips since the start of that year. My body didn't seem to 'snap' into the right tuck or pike shapes as it once did. I was finding that I couldn't get into my tight tuck shape quickly enough, and couldn't get enough height, so I was consistently landing short of rotation in the water – essentially, not completing enough somersaults before the water hit me and running out of room to complete the dive. What had clicked in the past with this dive just wasn't working for me anymore. For a time, one hip hurt more than the other, so I put more weight on one side, then my other hip started getting sore. Getting my legs off the board and into position was painful and slow; I just didn't have the same force behind me in my legs that I'd once had. As a result of trying to put more power through my legs for take-offs, and to get enough elevation into my dives, I was starting to suffer from sharp shooting pain in my shins.

The pain that I was experiencing during my running take-offs from my hips and my shins was excruciating. Having to run and push myself off the board with the right amount of force was awful; I felt like my legs were going to snap. It was a sharp targeted pain in the middle of my shin bone, which would radiate outwards and become dull and achy. My shins would throb in the night and this pulsing throb would keep me awake. I would lie there thinking about the fact that the next day I would have to get up and train that dive again and again. Obviously, the dive was not going well and I was struggling to 'make it', so I was forced to practise it more.

The run-up to that competition had not been easy and I had struggled in my training. There was even some question over whether I should compete at all. Jane had been unsure because I had had time off and I wasn't performing well. I argued that there was no difference between me doing the dives in training and at this competition. If there was any doubt in my mind before we arrived, by the time the plane had touched down on the tarmac in China, there was no question of me not taking part. I didn't want to just watch from the sidelines. I needed to be involved and part of the pack.

As I ran up the board, some of the normal pain that I felt in my shins was quelled by the adrenalin of being at an inter-national competition and diving alongside my fiercest rivals. In the warm-up sessions, my hips and shins had felt like hot pokers were being prodded against them but I was still determined to dive.

As I took off, a kind of numbness enveloped me. The take off felt freeze-frame slow and clumsy, but then suddenly I was plummeting fast towards the water. I felt really big and cumbersome in my shape, and like the G-force was pulling me even further away from my legs, and I was struggling to hold on. I couldn't squeeze tighter into my tuck shape, which would allow me to rotate more quickly, so I just had to go with it.

As I spun through the air, all I could think was, 'Well, this is going to hurt.'

There wasn't a bad 'flap' – where my body moves in unexpected ways – I just knew it would be so low-finishing that I wouldn't be able to get my hands out in front of me quickly enough to break my fall. Sure enough, when I landed in the water, my head took the brunt of the impact.

Smacking my head into the water at thirty-five miles per hour felt like something hard had punched my skull. It wasn't so much of a shock; I could sense it was coming, and having finished low so many times before in my diving practice, it never properly registered. I absorbed the hit and swallowed the fail, sinking into the water, swearing through the bubbles, then kicked myself to the surface. In any competition I never dwell on the last dive. You need to move on to the next one, so I bounded out of the pool in one clean motion. I still had one dive to go, so I did not look back.

It was only later that day in my hotel room that evening that I started to feel a bit strange. We were travelling straight from Beijing to Japan the next day for another leg of the World Series, and as we settled into our new environment for a few days of training before the competition, I felt weirdly jet-lagged and unmotivated. My limbs felt watery and weak and my brain was a bit fuzzy. In diving, you have precision-sharp awareness so you can spot where you are in the air, otherwise you can really hurt yourself, and my spatial awareness felt out.

I thought I was probably just tired from travelling. In the team, we are all pros at flying, travelling from A to B, getting onto coaches, being ferried about the place in a group, and defeating jet-lag, but the older I got, I was finding it less easy to bounce back. I competed in the ten-metre synchro with Dan Goodfellow, coming fourth, and then the mixed three-metre synchro competition with Grace Reid, winning a silver medal. The mixed synchro was a good result and was easier physically because we had been diving off the lower board, but I couldn't shake off the strange lethargy that I felt. I had said to Gareth, my physio, that I felt out of sorts and weary. I was also quite emotional and, in one training session before the individual competition, I found myself at the back of the board crying. I felt really overwhelmed and like I couldn't take the constant battering of my body. It was a low level of frustration that had been simmering for so long, and now felt like it was boiling up and over. I was struggling to even train at that point, let alone head into the competitions with a positive mindset.

'Let's just do a concussion test on you,' Gareth said. 'This just doesn't seem right.'

My score was enough to tip me towards doing computer tests. Every year we test our 'baseline' to check what our scores for various cognition tests would be on a normal day, and any assessment is judged against that. If you score slightly lower than your baseline that's fine, but I scored significantly lower. My reaction speed and short-term memory were way down.

'Yes, you have got a mild concussion, so you will not be diving in the individual event,' Garth said. 'It's too dangerous.'

I had had small concussions before then, and I imagine that I had probably suffered from many more of them in the past but hadn't even known.

My throat closed up and I felt a tightening in my chest. I knew it would not be safe to dive from the ten-metre board with a concussion, but it didn't stop me wanting to take part. I had dealt constantly with disappointments and frustrations in the past, of having to pull out of competitions due to injury, but it never gets easier. If I am in pain, I am in pain, but I always want to compete. The killer instinct to compete at all costs is so deep-seated and always has been. 2017 had been a really great career year for me, and I started to wonder whether that had been my peak. Should I just have quit whilst I was ahead? 2018 seemed to be going from bad to worse. The year had started badly, and I had been tired and constantly fatigued. I was struggling with my hips and now I had concussion. I would hate to feel like I was being forced out of my sport. Everyone wants to leave any sport on a high. It's a bit like a TV programme – you have to know when the last season should be, and not drag it on until people have stopped watching altogether and hate all the characters. Deep down, I knew this wasn't 'it' but it still smarted.

'OK,' I replied through gritted teeth. 'I understand.'

In the run-up to that competition, aside from my hips and shins, my general health had not been good. It started in October 2017; I had had a bit of a cold, but had woken up one morning with a real pain in my chest. I wondered, irrationally for a moment, if I could be having a heart attack because I had a horrible dull and painful sensation in my chest. But then I knew it wasn't my heart, because the pain was radiating from the wrong side of my chest. I was due to go and present the 'Best TV Show Award' at the Radio One Teen Awards and I had made a commitment. I would never normally pull out of any event; I approach all parts of my career in the same way as my diving, with the same work ethic. I hoped that if I continued with my day, the feelings might just pass. So I climbed out of bed to the shower and got myself together.

By the time I had made my way from home to the SSE Arena in Wembley, I was starting to feel really rough and dizzy and could feel a burning warm sensation rising through my neck to my head. By the time I walked to the arena, I could feel beads of sweat pooling at my lower back. I had some time, so I went over to the on-site paramedics and told them how I was feeling. I thought maybe they could give me a couple of paracetamol or something.

'Are you a little bit nervous about presenting the award?' one of the paramedics asked sympathetically, eyeing my smart attire.

'No, honestly, it's fine,' I replied. 'I give out these sorts of awards all the time.'

'I think you're having a panic attack.'

'Honestly, I know what panic attacks are and I don't think this is one. Genuinely, I think something else is wrong.'

'OK, let's just take your temperature and do your sats.'

She took out her thermometer and oximeter. She popped the thermometer in my ear, it beeped, and she glanced at it and then frowned. Then she took my oxygen levels with a pulse oximeter. My temperature was almost 39°c and my oxygen was hovering around 90 per cent.

'OK, your fever is sky high and your oxygen is low. I think we should take you to hospital.'

They whisked me to hospital in an ambulance, and I was immediately put on oxygen and on a drip. I felt relieved that

I wasn't on stage in front of thousands of people feeling that bad. I also felt a bit stupid for even thinking I could be up on stage in that condition. After some tests and a chest X-ray, the doctors immediately recognised it was pneumonia. I spent the day lying on my hospital bed in A&E, until my oxygen levels had stabilised. The medics sent me home with a hard-core course of antibiotics and with strict instructions to rest. With any respiratory illness, the more you train through it, the slower the recovery, so I knew I needed to get on board with the idea. I headed home to the sofa and tried to embrace it – I took about nine days off in the end. I then went through a phased return to training, where I didn't take on too much too quickly. After around a month I started to turn a corner, but the fatigue remained.

Heading into 2018, I still felt drained and devoid of any energy. Every single morning when my alarm started beeping, I scanned my body wondering what sort of day it would be and how I would get through it. Some days, even climbing out of bed and getting to the bathroom felt like a Herculean effort. I felt like I could sleep for a week and still be exhausted. The prospect of six hours of training every day felt over-whelming. It was a lingering fatigue that clung to me and seeped into everything. I just couldn't shake it off. I felt like I was doing everything right – sleeping enough, eating the right foods, focusing on recovery after each training session – but I still felt burnt out.

Externally, I was all smiles and trying to be my normal self but everything felt like it took 50 per cent more effort. What had been unchallenging before now felt hard. The fact I was struggling to muster the physical energy to train was draining my mental capacity to perform, like a sieve; the more I seemed to pour and the harder I tried, the more my body just wouldn't keep up. There was so much that I wanted to do but my body just wasn't keeping in step with my normal programme.

I wondered if there could be an underlying problem, maybe something that was not obvious that was making me feel so bad? I did some blood tests, but they didn't show anything. In the end, I went to see my doctor, who is based at the Institute of Sport, Exercise and Health (ISEH) on Tottenham Court Road.

I explained to him how I felt and how exhaustion seemed to pervade every part of my body. It didn't take long for him to deliver his diagnosis.

He said: 'I have seen this in lots of athletes your age. You are not necessarily coming to the end of your career but you are very much a mature athlete.'

It felt crazy that just a few years beforehand I was one of the youngest athletes, who rarely struggled with injury. I was like Tigger, with boundless energy, and would look at the older divers who were always straight up onto the physio bed after every competition, and I wondered what was wrong with them. Suddenly that 'older' person was me.

I was only 23 and starting to feel like the grandad of the sport very quickly.

'I think you have over-training syndrome,' he continued. 'You have trained hard for so many years and you've been going non-stop and working so hard. There comes a point where your body is telling you that it needs a break.

'You need to take some proper time off.'

As an athlete, it is very hard to know when to have some downtime. Jane, who trained in the Russian system, was used to her athletes continually training, and I think she probably felt like it was in my head. My doctor told her that even if it was in my head, I needed some respite.

Other athletes, especially the Chinese, train to their limits and beyond. They are a force to be reckoned with on the world stage. The Chinese train their divers from the ages of four or five in intense state sports schools, where they are looking for the next medal winner. There is not normal school as we know it in the educational sense – the aim of school is simply about being the best diver in the world and the military-style training is brutal. If anyone does not try hard enough, they are simply replaced because there are so many waiting in the wings for their moment. They are like robots in their consistency, and there is a ruthless focus on the sports that play to their strengths. By 12, they are living at their school, training for seven hours a day, seven days a week. It is part of a pyramid system that is looking for that one in a billion. The rewards for the Chinese when they win are huge, and it brings status, riches and power. This is what I am up against. To jump higher, be stronger and win more medals always comes at the expense of the athlete's health. Perseverance and resolve is considered the benchmark. Sometimes it's not just the system that pushes an athlete, they are just as demanding of themselves. You need to and have to want to keep pushing through. I know I have been guilty of this many times, but to compete with the best in the world you have to train like them. It's a tricky balance.

I am used to my training schedule, but the level of intensity can be gruelling. My training ebbs and flows over time, depending on which part of the year I am training in, and the competitions I have approaching. After any time off, we move on to strength and endurance work in the gym. The gym sessions become harder and more intense. This is then balanced out with slightly easier pool sessions. In the run-up to important competitions, with the strength work in place and the power we need to perform our dives, the pool training then becomes increasingly vigorous, with more frequent dives from ten metres to practise our set, which is physically more taxing.

A typical day of training for me might start with an hour and a quarter in the gym doing diving conditioning exercises, weights, and dry land somersaults. This will be followed by an hour and a quarter diving in the pool, completing countless dives from the different boards, analysing my performance, bettering each one.

Then after lunch, I will go back to the gym and dry board area for another hour and a quarter of gymnastics conditioning training, a dry land diving specific workout, or a gymnastics tumbling session followed by another hour and a quarter in the pool. Then I may do spinning, yoga, gyrotonics, and twice a week I have a massage after training. For over a decade, with the odd exception, I had trained for six hours, six days a week. I never wake up without some sort of throbbing ache, shooting pain or sharp twinge. But that's the job, so you just get on with it.

Of course, aside from the general risk of overdoing it and causing injuries over time, there are countless ways you can injure yourself suddenly. The force of any impact is enough to break bones, detach your retinas, burst your eardrums or dislocate joints. There is always the risk of jumping too close to the board on reverse and inward dives and slamming your head on the board. Scalp lacerations are common and I have seen divers knock themselves unconscious from doing this, and having to be pulled out of the pool by other divers or lifeguards. Diving is considered a collision sport. One way to avoid the worst injuries is by using a bubble machine in the water, which decreases the surface tension, and we often use this in training when learning new dives. It moves the surface of the water, so we can see it more clearly when we are spinning round. This, in turn, can help us gauge how far we are from the water during spins and somersaults, which helps us perfect our dives. In London, we also use water sprays, which make the water even clearer to 'spot'.

I can always tell if I am spinning too fast or too slow, or if I have not quite grabbed my legs properly, or if I am slightly off balance. Things can also go wrong in mid-air or upon entry to the water. Most of the time you can tell it's going to go wrong well before you hit the water, and those milliseconds before impact are never enjoyable. If you are not completely tight and straight and connected with your whole body, any dive can go all over the place. I have had many times when my head has gone one way and my body the other way, cricking my neck so I haven't been able to move it for a few days. My arms have often buckled as they hit the water, so I have woken up the next day and been unable to straighten my arms, or been able to straighten one but not the other. Sometimes my back hurts from twisting, arching and extending. Even when dives are perfectly executed, injuries can happen.

Coming back to training gradually after my concussion injury in Beijing, my hips and shins continued to play up. I felt like I was in pain around the clock, and there was no respite from it. Every time I took off to practise my front four and a half somersaults, the hard impact of the take off from the end of the board was agonising, and a dark, stabbing pain rippled through my legs for hours afterwards. Some days, even walking produced a nauseating and dull throbbing deep in my legs and hips. It felt punishing.

Training towards the Commonwealth Games in July 2018, I was in agony. I worked closely with Gareth and had regular massages and ice baths, and completed more stretching and mobilisation work. I focused hard on ways I could help myself, but the pain dug its teeth in. I had lots of MRI scans, because whatever we did, the pain persisted. We found out that my hips are fused in such a way that the ball does not move in the socket properly, because my hip is the wrong shape, so does not allow me the full hip movement range. I had micro-tears in my hips, and this adjusted the way that I was diving. There was some discussion about whether I should have surgery to scrape away some of the bone to make it rounder, but the stakes seemed too high; along with the weeks of recovery and rehabilitation involved in undergoing major surgery, there are occasions when it is not always successful, or could even make the situation worse.

As the quality of my dives went down, so the more I dived to try to improve my performance. It was a vicious cycle of pushing myself further and further to try to improve, but the gains were miniscule, and then I would dive badly again.

The Commonwealth Games has always been one of my favourite competitions. In 2010, when I was just 16, I had won both the individual ten-metre gold and the synchro. It had been one of my first big international wins. I had also won the individual event again in 2014 in Glasgow, so winning the event the third time felt incredibly important to me. I was determined to dive at the event, which was being held on the Gold Coast, in Australia.

In the lead-up to the competition, I was even slower getting my dives back than I had been after my concussion. I was on the cusp of a decision as to whether I would dive at all, but I continued to train as hard as I could manage. I wasn't making any of the dives – everything was low-finishing or not right – and everything felt extremely difficult. I spoke to Lance a few times, voicing my fears and worries that I just couldn't do it. He kept telling me it was fine.

'No, you're not listening,' I kept muttering. 'I don't think you understand. This is not going to be good.'

As well as my front four and a half, I was struggling with my front Firework Twister because it was also a running take-off and needed the same amount of impact. During training one session, I went to grab my legs and missed; I was forced to bail out halfway through and landed with an uncomfortable whack on my side.

In the end, it felt like the only way forwards was for me to pull out of the individual competition. Again, the disappointment stung. I was still competing in the synchro, so I was determined to do well in that competition and put everything I had left into it. It was my one and only chance. Due to the pain I was experiencing, I had another scan on my shins. It clearly showed that the stress responses were so bad, it was at the point that they could develop into stress fractures. I was pretty shocked to hear that, and I wondered what that would even mean for my diving career. I was told to wear Moon Boots all the time, except for when I was competing.

Psychologically, it was pretty rough. I was turning up at the pool walking with my crutches, with Moon Boots strapped on both legs, hobbling along like some sort of premature geriatric. Then I would take them off and stash them to one side and be expected to complete those hardcore running take-offs. Now, I wonder if it was sheer lunacy my being in such a bad way, yet still with the determination to compete. Physically, I was miles off where I should have been. I was doubtful of my ability and I felt very self-conscious.

Going into the ten-metre synchro, my partner Dan Goodfellow and I – normally and without injury – should have been able to win the competition relatively easily, but it certainly was not ours for the taking. The other English duo, Matthew Dixon and Noah Williams, were strong competitors, as were the Australian divers, Domonic Bedggood and Dec Stacey. I also knew I would have to compete my front four and a half, and that I had not done a good front four and a half for that whole year. However, this was Dan's best dive, so I hoped he would carry me if I did a bad one and bring our points back up, so we could come out on top.

I didn't train it in the warm-up and didn't do all the normal lead-ups in training; I did not have enough strength in my shins. It was the final dive on our list, and going into that round, the points were close, so it was a make-or-break dive.

The whistle blew and it was just Dan and I together, standing at the back of the board in the open air.

'Ready?'

'Yes.'

'One, two, three, go . . .'

Running down the board, I remember thinking, 'Well if there's ever a time to say "fuck it", it's now. Even if my shins snap on the take off, it's my last shot.' I wanted, needed, demanded to give it everything, regardless of the pain. I wanted to win at all costs and that desire swept over me anaesthetising any feelings of pain. My whole body was pumping with so much adrenalin that my legs and hips felt completely numb. In that moment I didn't care about the consequences, the agony, the lasting effects. The desire to win and win at all costs seemed to overtake every faculty.

As I got into my tuck shape, I could feel that it was one of the better tucks shapes I had got into all year.

'This is my only chance,' I thought. 'I cannot throw it away.'

Punching the water with my arms outstretched, I knew it had been a great dive. I felt sucked into that splashless vacuum I know so well. It was the best front four and a half that I had done all year.

Unfortunately, Dan's dive had not gone to plan and he had finished low, but we still got enough points to win the gold medal. Climbing out of the pool, there were a lot of surprised and wide-eyed faces. The Australian, Malaysian and one of the other English coaches all came up to me afterwards and asked how on earth I had done it.

'You've been landing on your face all week and then put in that dive?' they laughed. 'How did you pull that dive out of your arse? Fair play to you.'

It was a year of hell; mishap after mishap, but knowing that the Commonwealth Games was my target saw me through. It was probably the most challenging competition of my career. In any other job, if anyone had the kind of ailments that I was suffering from, they would take time off to heal, but in sport things are different. Looking back now, it seems miraculous that we managed to win a gold medal.

After that competition, eating outside a restaurant in the sun with Lance, I took a step back and looked at where I was in my life. I had been married for a year, and Robbie, our son, was on the way. At that competition, I had also faced the issue of my sexuality head-on, and spoken out about the fact that in thirty-seven out of the fifty-three Commonwealth countries homosexuality was illegal. It had been forty-three countries four years previously – change was coming. It felt good to use my platform to call for positive progress.

I was due to travel to Kazan in Russia for another leg of the World Series, before the World Cup a few weeks later in Wuhan in June. Originally, I had planned to take part in both competitions, before travelling out to Los Angeles to be there for the birth of my son. He was due in late June.

To continue going for competition after competition, with the injuries I was suffering from and pushing through, suddenly seemed like madness. I was in agony and it felt like a constant battle to get myself to the pool to train through the pain. Did I come back after my concussions and tiredness when I was ready and felt better, or because I wanted to train in the competitions? Looking back, I know it was for the latter reason. I had pushed myself too fast and too soon and made mistakes.

I voiced my plan to take six weeks off from diving, and Gareth agreed. For a physio, it is always a balance between optimising my performance and condition to win medals, whilst minimising any risk of injury. He needed to just get me through each competition in one piece, but we were running out of options. The fact that the Moon Boots were now my choice of footwear made it seem like the time to evaluate my position. To be one of the world's best you have to train like the world's best, and hobbling around the pool edge was not going to cut it.

I knew I needed to let my bones heal so I could come back stronger, fitter and healthier than before. I knew my years were limited, so I needed to look at the bigger picture. The Tokyo Olympics at that stage were just two years away. My body would be completely broken by 2020 if I continued to dive and train in the same way. I wanted to get better and be better. Everyone was in agreement; Jane and Alexei said we would figure out what was next once my bones were healed and I felt strong enough to return.

The thought that I needed that amount of time off was also quite nerve-wracking. I wondered what I would do without training to keep me busy. In the end, that break was the best thing that I have done in my whole diving career. It allowed me another chance to reset and to see where my priorities were in my life. It was also a really magical time on a personal level, and allowed Lance and I to have some time together before Robbie was born. To take the diving out of my life before his birth took away so much of the stress and allowed us to prepare mentally to be parents. It also gave me a sense of what mattered most.

Despite the break from diving, I was still aware of keeping my condition up and staying fit, so my return to training and competing went smoothly. When my hips started hurting, Gareth had suggested that I tried gyrotonics; a mixture of Pilates, yoga, dance, t'ai chi, swimming and gymnastics. It uses frames, rotational discs, and pulleys, and is a mixture of complex movements that are three-dimensional, slow and segmented, and completed with different levels of tension. I think this is the exercise that saved me and fixed my body, because of its ability to engage all the small muscles and increase joint mobility and range of movement. Unlike some other forms of exercise, it can be highly personalised, and looks at your individual body as a whole, rather than tackling each problem in isolation. I spent a lot of time doing gyrotonics, and since then have swapped out one dry land diving session for one of these tailored sessions in my daily training routine. There was a time where I would scoff at gyrotonics or yoga – it seemed a bit wet and boring. But now I have learned to believe in people who think they can help me, because often they can. I have learned that actually slowing down and taking a step back can really make the biggest difference over the long-term. Gyrotonics has really improved my conditioning; Tisha Harrington from Kings Cross Studio has been helping me on that journey. Since then, I have had no problems in my hips and back; my flexibility has improved; and many of the small niggles that plagued me before then have been solved. I recognised what I needed to do as a mature athlete, and it allowed me to work with my body rather than hammer it to death. I wanted to take time for myself to re-balance and centre my body. I wanted to get back to doing exercise that I really enjoyed. I wanted to take my mind completely away from diving, so I didn't do any of the normal training that I would do in the gym when I was diving, and instead went to fun spin group workout classes, yoga classes, and on long shirtless hikes in the LA countryside with Lance. I found that walking out in the open allowed me to clear my head and be more mindful. The amazing glow of the sun and the opportunity to head to trail tracks so near the city and talk about life is one of the things that Lance and I miss most about being in California.

Before long, Robbie was here and I was suddenly a parent, and it became even more important that I was looking after my body. I didn't want to be the dad in the playground limping around due to bad legs, or unable to engage in the same way because I was concussed. I wanted to be there for every single precious moment. Yes, diving was and is important, but my family will always be my first priority.

Going back to training in August 2018, I felt really refreshed and ready. It was the least sore I had ever been and where I had the most range of motion. It was the first time I had properly taken time off and really concentrated on getting over my injury and looking after my body and my mental health. I felt a sense of peace, calm and togetherness in a way that I hadn't before. At the time, I thought I only had a year and a half left of professional diving until the 2020 Olympics, and I felt content. The sense of pressure had dissipated, and once again I decided that I was there for the ride because I enjoyed it.

Injuries are just an unfortunate part of training, and good health is always a priority. It is a balance between pushing yourself hard enough, and not getting injured. Even now, nearly twenty years after I first started diving, I am still learning how to manage load and volume in order to avoid injury, but it is a continual work in progress. I am still learning what my body can manage, what I can handle, what is too much and too little. I know I will be continuing to learn all the way until the very end of my career, and even then I won't know half of what I could know. I have learned that I can't endlessly push my body to the edge of what is physically and mentally possible.

Sometimes the psychological impact of injury and being ill is worse than the physical aspect. I have learned over time to never neglect my mental health during the recovery process. Injury can make you feel helpless, and knowing there is only so much you can do to speed up the healing process is very important. I know now to never skip the rehab process because it is boring, and I try not to push myself before I am ready. I try to focus on the positives of what I have and will learn from them, and always look forwards. I know I can deal with whatever is on the other side of any injury or illness. I always look at the end goal.

CONFIDENCE

Despite having spent most of my childhood wearing only swimming trunks, and being photographed that way for many national newspapers to boot, like most kids I didn't consider how I looked at all. I was always well built but never had to worry about what I ate because, between growing and training so much, I was burning a lot of calories. Food played a big part of our family life. Every Wednesday night, we went for a curry with my dad and grandparents after training, and Mum always cooked proper meals for us. For a long time, Sunday was my only day off; Sunday lunch was a ritual for our family and there was always a crowd around the table. As a child, everyone that I trained with focused on diving – none of us made comments about how each other looked. But, despite having always found it easy to eat a lot and not put on any weight, as I started getting older, I started to lose the ability to be a human garbage disposal, and began to fill out more.

In December 2011, when I was 17, we were on a training camp in Adelaide. We often spent a couple of weeks in the sun over the winter months to get some vitamin D and train in the outside pools.

The Team GB doctor came up to me one day after training.

'Tom can I have a little chat with you for a minute?'

'Yeah, sure,' I said, wondering what I had done wrong, or what she might say.

'Alexei pulled me aside and asked me to have a conversation with you about your weight,' she said.

'Right, what about it?' I asked, slightly baffled as to where the conversation was headed.

'He just wants to weigh you and see where you are. We want to try and help you lose some weight.'

'Wait a sec. What?' I was genuinely confused. Up until that point, it had never occurred to me that there could be anything wrong with my weight. I ate well and I trained hard. The irony was that the diving team and I had been filming a jokey lip-synch video to LMFAO's 'Sexy and I Know It' on the beach when we were not training. I thought I was fine and looked good enough.

It was the first time I had considered that I could be fat, out of shape, or even the 'right' shape, whatever that was. I had spent half my life half-naked up until that point, and yet it was the first time I felt really exposed.

It occurred to me in a horrible rush that I wasn't being judged just on my diving ability; I was also being appraised when I stood on the diving board for how I looked or how skinny or fat I was.

The GB diving team had basic nutrition workshops in the run-up to the Olympics in 2008, but most of the time the nutritionists had told me I didn't need to worry and that I was in good shape. There had been no mention of my weight since then. I was burning off between 3,000 and 4,000 calories a day training, so I had always just eaten what I thought was right to give me enough energy to dive.

I had no idea what to say and do. After the chat, I felt so awkward. They said they would help me to lose weight, but they hadn't given me any advice. My natural reaction was to try and joke about it, so when we were at the breakfast bar I would quip, 'Just lettuce leaves for me please!'

The reality was that I had really taken what the doctor had said to heart. The next day, I started a new routine of getting up earlier than the rest of the team to do loads of cardio in the gym, and eating less. No one noticed my change in routine. Even in the space of a few days I began to notice a difference; my clothes felt a bit looser. I was beginning to lose weight and it made me feel good and like I was achieving what I needed to.

It was so triggering for me. That conversation happened just before Christmas and on my return home, I vowed to continue to lose weight. I remember that year around the dinner table, I cut out all carbohydrates and reduced my portion sizes. My new quest had very little to do with being healthy and optimising my training, and everything to do with my appearance. Whilst my brothers loaded up on roast potatoes, sausage rolls, Christmas pudding and mince pies with abandon, I nibbled on turkey and a few Brussels sprouts. It may seem remarkable, but even in the run-up to the London Olympics there simply wasn't anyone on the team who could give me proper nutritional advice because there just is not enough money in the sport to pay for this level of expertise, so I did what I thought could work from the things I'd read or seen on TV. I started doing faddy stuff like skipping breakfast, not eating for whole days, or cutting out whole food groups. There has always been such a focus on diet culture in traditional media, so on some level, my new quest to lose weight seemed completely normal. My eating was not healthy by a long stretch. Within a month, though, I had lost five kilos, so as far as I was concerned, I was making a success of it.

Having worked with proper sports nutritionists since then, who I met through Jane, I now know that weight is not a measure of how in shape you are; this is predicated on how much of a percentage of your body is fat. Your weight is not an indication of overall health. In the US college system where

From the age of 7, when I started diving, Dad would drive me to all of my training sessions and competitions around the country. He was my biggest supporter.

DARREN JACK/SHUTTERSTOCK

CLIVE ROSE/STAFF/GETTY IMAGES SPORT GETTY IMAGES

Left: the moment in which I had to ask the referee for a re-dive following a camera flash during my 'Twister' at the London 2012 Olympics. My coach, Andy, stands behind me.

Below: I was so thrilled to win a bronze medal at the 2012 Olympic Games. I was 18 and on the cusp of adulthood, freedom and independence.

CLIVE ROSE/STAFF/GETTY IMAGES SPORT GETTY IMAGES

Left: arriving at the Nickelodeon Kids' Choice Awards in LA, 2013, where I had won the 'Favourite UK Sports Star' award. It was after this event that I first met Lance and instantly fell in love.

Below: being interviewed by Jonathan Ross in December 2013, after I had created my coming out video and told everyone that I was in a relationship with Lance.

Teaching former Boyzone singer Keith Duffy how to dive from the three-metre board on one of the *Splash!* training sessions in 2014.

Filming *Tom Daley Goes Global* for ITV2 with my best friend, Sophie, in 2014, in Switzerland (right) and Morocco (below). I felt so guilty for taking time off from training, but reasoned that filming the series was like having a six-week gap year.

Left: competing my 'Firework' at the 2015 FINA World Series in London; this was the first time after the 2012 Olympics that I truly began to feel like a champion again.

Below: diving an inward piked half somersault with Dan Goodfellow at the Men's Synchronised 10-metre Platform final at the Rio 2016 Olympics.

Dan and I eagerly awaiting the result of the Men's Synchronised 10-metre Platform final in Rio, unsure whether our final dive had been enough to clinch the bronze. We were overjoyed when our score flashed up.

Being comforted by my coach, Jane, following my performance in the Men's 10-metre Platform semi-final at the 2016 Olympic Games.

Above: me and Lance on our wedding day, with my best friend Sophie, cousins Sam, Malia, and Brooke, and Lance's brother Todd and best friend Ryan. My eyes filled with tears as Lance approached me, it was one of the happiest days of my life.

Above: Lance and I holding our baby boy, Robbie Ray Black-Daley, feeling nothing but joy.

Right: the picture that Lance and I used to announce the birth of our baby, Robbie, to the world.

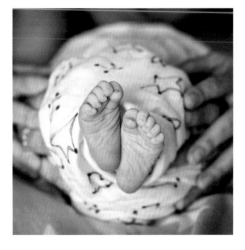

Competing a reverse tucked three and a half somersault in the Men's Synchronised 10-metre Platform final at the Tokyo 2020 Olympic Games with Matty Lee.

The moment in which Matty, Jane and I realised that we had won a gold medal. Having competed in four Olympics, and waited 13 years for this moment, I was blown away.

Knitting before the Men's 10-metre Platform final at the Tokyo 2020 Olympic Games. Knitting really helped to keep me sane at these Games, and got lots of media attention, too!

Receiving my bronze medal for the 10-metre Platform at the Tokyo 2020 Olympic Games, and becoming the first British diver to ever win four medals at the Olympics.

Jane had worked, there were people who specialised in this and could help. It is commonplace for athletes to have support around the food they eat, and have their bodies analysed in a more sophisticated way. But at that time I was judged solely by the numbers on the scales. Strangely, it didn't seem to affect my sporting performance, or my ability to keep diving well, but I felt like crap all the time. I had no energy, and after years of blissful ignorance, I felt incredibly self-conscious about my body. Every time I stripped off, I wondered if someone was looking at me, thinking I was overweight. It felt like a rain cloud of negative speak that followed me around.

Some days, I would go into our gymnastics training and our Ukrainian coach would bark, 'Get on the scales.' Though none of the coaches talked openly about my weight with me, or with each other in front of me, I think he had been told to keep an eye on my weight. I was still painfully aware that I was considered overweight.

I would walk over in front of all my fellow divers, feeling panic rise in my chest and wondering why I had been singled out amongst all the others for that form of special treatment. Standing there exposed and watching the numbers scatter upwards was such a deflating experience. I think there was an assumption that because I was a man I wouldn't be both-ered by it. There was no sensitivity whatsoever in how my weight was talked about.

This coach would make me do extra cardio when I had finished training, to keep my weight down. He and Alexei were very close, and I felt as though he was the eyes and ears on the ground to ensure my weight was being constantly monitored, and that I knew about it.

It seemed there was an expectation of how everyone thought I should look that I wasn't quite meeting. My anxiety around it spiralled and it was as if my brain had been hijacked by worry and its trusty sidekick, fear. I started to zero in on what I considered imperfections in my body. At times when I took my top off by the side of the pool or got ready to dive, even if there were not loads of people around, I wondered if everyone was just thinking about how I looked. It was almost paralysing.

In the run-up to the London 2012 Olympics, I did not eat properly and considerably under-fuelled myself. I always had horrendous guilt if I ate what I considered a treat, like a Chinese takeaway or a dessert. On some days, when I felt like I had ordered too much when we went out for dinner, or I thought that a piece of cake I had eaten was too big, I would make myself throw up. Any time I ate anything that made me feel good, a huge cloud of guilt would wash over me. I would be so disgusted with myself. I knew in my rational brain that I shouldn't be doing it, but a voice in my head would tell me I was getting fat and would gain weight from what I had eaten, and it seemed to drown everything else out.

It felt like the only way I could feel better was to get rid of the food that I 'shouldn't' have eaten, but the feelings of relief were short-lived because they were quickly followed by waves of shame and remorse. Or it would go the other way and I would starve myself for the whole of the day after eating something I felt I shouldn't have. Some days I relished the fact I wasn't hungry, or would just avoid eating much at all. I would drink Diet Coke and eat sugar-free Polos, or crunch on ice to try to trick my body into thinking that I was eating something solid. Resolving to simply not eat sometimes was easier. I wondered if I should talk to someone and tell them how I was feeling, but we had a lot going on at home, so I kept it to myself. Those emotions were only amplified by careless comments about my weight as the Olympic Games approached.

I found out that Alexei was showing pictures of me to my coaches, telling them that I needed to look a certain way – how I had looked when I was in Beijing when I was 14 years old. Alexei had his eyes on all of the divers, and he clearly thought I looked skinny and moved in a way he saw as optimal for my sport, but I was also practically still a child, all lanky limbs and big teeth. Sport can be like any other job and like any office grapevine, his words worked their way back to me.

Two days before the individual competition at the Olympics, I was sitting outside in the village with some of the other divers. It was lunchtime and I had a chicken wrap in my hand.

'Should you be eating that?' Alexei asked as he walked past, with a look of disdain on his face.

I was really shocked but for once, I felt strong. The fact he had said this to my face as I was getting ready for the biggest competition of my life made me feel so angry. I knew I needed to eat to fuel myself. Even in my head at the time, a chicken wrap felt like a good choice.

'Yes, it's my lunch,' I said, quietly fuming. 'I'm going to eat this today.'

I started off at 76 kilos at the end of 2011 and competed at the 2012 Olympics at 67 kilos. I lost a considerable amount of weight over that time, but negative thoughts continued to inform my eating and I felt constantly hungry and was often exhausted. In the pool, I ran out of energy quicker than I had when I'd been fuelling myself properly, and yet despite all of these negative side effects, no one considered that my weight loss was not a good thing.

The prelims of the Olympic Games had gone badly and that evening, something clicked. I knew I needed to eat enough to have enough energy to see the competition through. I decided to just eat properly. I had been training for this competition my whole life, it was unlikely that I was ever going to get to compete in an Olympics again in front of a home crowd; I couldn't throw away my chance at a medal because I hadn't eaten any breakfast. My habits changed overnight. I resolved that I'd eat well throughout the rest of the competition, and I often munched on gummy bears on the poolside. I wanted, and needed, the energy, so I could dive and sustain my performance. My drive to succeed had finally managed to outweigh the pressure that was being placed on me to adapt my body image. I understand now that, much like cars are for Formula One drivers, our bodies are the main tool of success for athletes. If they are too heavy or too light, then we will not be performing at our best. Unlike in F1, though, where there is a team of experts working on the car, there was no help for me.

Just before the final competition, Alexei walked over and said: 'Just so you know, if we don't win a medal today, we get no funding.' It didn't make me feel great and I wondered why he had said it.

Looking back, he treated me like a child he needed to teach, about both my weight and performance. Maybe that was his idea of a motivational talk. After I won my medal, he treated me with a new level of respect. It was as if I had grown into a man in his eyes. Many sporting professionals do not know how to handle the issue of weight, or what happens when someone becomes out of shape. There is pressure from all angles to be slim, and opinions about how I look and its importance is never far away. There is a sense that in the same way that people can tell you to improve your performance, they can also just tell you that you are overweight and that you can work harder in order to lose it, disregarding the mental toll that speaking about our bodies in this way can have. Like everything, it is not just the physical side of weight that needs to be addressed but the mental one too. Even now, if I have a bad day at training or I feel slow or sluggish for any reason, Jane will put it down to the fact that I have put on weight or I am 'a bit heavy'. Often this is not the case at all, and the way that it's conveyed to me makes me feel rubbish about myself. Many coaches also believe that if you look ripped up on the board, the judges will automatically be on your side. For a long time, Jane told me to wear black trunks because they were slimming. When the Olympic trunks came out and there was a white pair, she told me to choose the navy version.

I never made myself sick again after the London Olympics and I've learned so much more about proper nutrition and what I should be eating. It was a revelation when in 2013 Jane introduced me to a proper nutritionist, and she gave me a meal-planner.

'Wait, you are telling me I can eat all this?' I said.

The list of foods in front of me looked more like something I would eat in a week not every day.

The nutritionist told me it wasn't just about what I was eating but when I was eating, the macronutrients in everything I ate, how I was fuelling before and after training, and how food can affect my performance and recovery. Before then, I had always thought that I should never eat after a workout because I would undo all my hard work. I was taught that this is exactly the opposite of what I should've been doing, and taking on some protein within twenty minutes to refuel and repair was essential in order to get anything out of the workout at all. I learned more about how to prep meals, not to limit my calories, and how to make the right food choices during normal training days, on my days off and before competitions. This knowledge was very empowering.

I also did a proper body fat scan when I started working with Jane. The average male body fat percentage is 18 to 24 per cent. The first 'bod pod' that I did, I had 10 per cent body fat, and I felt I needed to cut down from that. You have to be below 12 per cent to see abs, and 10 per cent body fat in diving is apparently too fat for the sport. A year later in 2014 I had another similar type of scan. It was just before I left for the World Cup in Shanghai, and my fat percentage was down to 3 per cent. I had been training really hard, and even though I had stopped making myself sick and had stopped doing the 'faddy' stuff, I was definitely maintaining a calorie deficit, where I was expending more calories than I was consuming. Although it felt great to see that number, I was also really struggling with energy, concentration, and was getting injuries. To maintain that body composition, I would have to be in a calorie deficit all the time, and it felt impossible to maintain. I was barely eating anything and training hard; it felt brutal and was not sustainable for me. Now, I have worked out that I feel my best when I am around 7–8 per cent body fat even though I still feel a pressure to stay slim. While elite athletes need to have very low body fat indeed, this doesn't apply to everyone, and the Royal College of Nursing lists 8–20 per cent body fat as ideal for 20- to 39-year-old men.

My body image has improved, but feelings around food and guilt often still persist. Ever since that conversation in Australia I have weighed myself every single morning. I even take my own scales away with me when I go on training camps and to competitions. I don't know any other diver who does that. I know that it probably isn't good for me to keep weighing myself, but whilst I am still diving, it is part of my routine. I do feel like I judge myself based on what my weight is every single day. As I have got older, I understand that there are many more factors to your weight than just how much fat you are carrying, such as how hydrated you are, how much you are training (this can increase water retention through inflammation) and how much carbohydrate or glycogen you are storing in your muscles or liver. Education has helped me comprehend that. But once you experience body image issues and struggles with your self-esteem, it is very hard to change or shrug off that way of thinking. It becomes so ingrained and entrenched; it feels like part of me now.

Before we leave for any competition, we are always weighed. In previous years, I have always tried to hit a certain number before a competition, thinking that if I succeed in being a certain weight then I will dive well. There is not enough funding in the sport to do body fat testing before we leave for every competition; instead, there is a fairly crude test to measure our body fat using callipers to literally measure the thickness of fat under our skin on various parts of our bodies, such as our triceps, torso and abdomen. Out of all the boys of the elite team that I train with, I am the heaviest and have the highest skin fold. So I am nearly always left somewhat disheartened after these tests.

Should be, could be, slimmer.

Obviously, problems surrounding weight are not always linked to a lack of support. There are always background voices expressing an opinion about how you look, even if it is not to your face, or meant badly or in a negative way. They echo and bounce around for a long time after any conversation or casual comment. That one conversation in Australia still comes back to me when I eat something that I think that I 'shouldn't' now; I find myself looking in the mirror and thinking, 'Oh gosh, I shouldn't have eaten that . . .' If I've had a particularly big dinner, or think that I've eaten too much, I won't let Lance cuddle me or touch my stomach in bed. I feel too exposed.

I think that the lingering hangover of trying to be the right size will be with me forever, but I always try to work through these feelings in my head and be more confident in my own image. I try to catch myself having these negative thoughts and tell myself that I am doing the right thing and eating the right things, but it's tough. People's bodies change over time. It is never a good idea to compare yourself with others, or your younger self. No one has the same body as the next person, so everyone is going to look different.

I try hard to focus on how I feel, regardless of how heavy I am. I have also learned that looking my best and performing my best don't necessarily tally. When I performed at the Olympics in Rio in 2016, I weighed 71 kilos. I won the prelim round but failed to make it through the semi-finals and crashed out of the event. A year later, at the World Championships in Budapest where I won, beating the Olympic medallists, I was 73 kilos. It goes to show that while I may have looked great in 2016, and dived well for part of the competition, I did not have the endurance to maintain the level of energy and strength I needed to continue to dive at competition level on consecutive days. In 2017, I was heavier but also stronger, with the stamina I needed to compete for three days straight in different competitions. I could never perform with the level of endurance that I needed when I was not consuming enough calories.

How I feel and how I am able to perform matters most. I need to be confident in how I look, but I now understand more about how to fuel my body and my brain and prepare myself properly for what I need to do. And, crucially, I shouldn't listen to others' opinions about how I look.

RESILIENCE

From a young age, I've had a resilient and determined mindset when it has come to my sport. If anyone says I can't do something, well . . . I'll show them I can. I'll just work harder in order to get better. Simple.

When I started to compete as a youngster, I began to be noticed by people within the sport. At one National Novice competition in April 2003, when I was a month shy of my ninth birthday, I was spotted by a lady called Chelsea Warr who ran a National Lottery-funded programme for divers around the UK called World Class Start; Chelsea coached a group of divers that she thought had potential to achieve international success as part of this. The people who had ranked in the top five in that competition – of which I was one – were put through a series of simple tests, such as doing a tuck jump, a pike shape and a sprint test. She also measured how long my legs were compared to my upper body and the length of my arms.

I started to go to training camps with other divers from around the country; there were nine camps each year. We started to be funnelled away from our regional training hubs to form a junior national team, and the competition was stiff. It was here I met Jack Laugher, Alicia Blagg, Grace Reid, and some of the other divers who I have spent the last decade competing alongside.

Part of these camps included what was called talent testing. This involved a series of detailed tests designed to spot those of us who had the greatest potential to succeed in the long-term. I failed every single step of these tests, from flexibility to strength and jump height. I could never do the splits, and was simply not as good as some of the other divers there.

I started to get used to coaches and other people talking openly about what they considered to be my ability in the pool.

One of the top coaches told me outright: 'You are never going to make it as a top diver.' At the time, the best and strongest boys were doing a 'pike list' from a three-metre board, and she told me I would never be able to do it because I wasn't flexible enough, or strong enough, and didn't have good enough technique.

Instead of feeling deflated, I remember walking away from

that exchange feeling stronger. It was like that coach had given me more determination to succeed; I had to show her that I was capable. This particular coach had a diver going through the same programme, who I competed with closely. He was always better than me and always came out slightly ahead of me in most of the tests. Beating him was what I soon became fixated on. No matter how many times I was told I wasn't going to be able to do it, I let the comments wash over me. Nothing was going to stop me from fulfilling my dream.

I now realise that I was lucky that Chelsea saw something in me, and in Jack – who was also not at the top of these talent tests either – that no one else did, and refrained from dropping us from the team despite the fact that our scores indicated that we wouldn't make it. Yes, we were not like the gymnasts who could open their legs to 180 degrees on demand. Perhaps we were not as strong or flexible as some of the others. I don't know whether it was our attitude or how hard we tried to make our moves as good as everyone else's even when they weren't, but she continued to see our potential. She later told me that she saw I had something else that other people did not have: in the pool, I had all the spatial awareness and ability to 'spot' that I needed to be a top diver.

Slowly but surely, I started to rise above the competition in the pool, leaving the other divers in my wake. My progress quickly outstripped theirs. However, my testing results were still not the best. However hard I tried to master the splits I never did quite manage it, but the movements I needed to help me in the pool to be a better diver, like hanging pike-ups, where you hang from the wall bars and lift your legs up to touch your toes on the bar with straight legs, and jump height, did improve. If potential was solely judged by these tests, neither Jack nor I would have made it as divers. Resilience is important; it ensures that you keep going, even when everyone else believes that you should quit. And who knows what you'll achieve when you refuse to be beaten.

Media coverage around my life started around this time. Coming home from a training session with Dad in his van one day, I spotted the local newspaper, the *Plymouth Herald*, sitting on one of the fabric seats. I was 9 and by then, I was training at the Mayflower Centre three times a week and going on these World Class Start weekend training camps. I was obsessed with diving and was completely single-minded in my attempts to master new dives and better my performance each week. There in the paper was a picture of some of my diving friends, who had just been to the Nationals. There was a small piece of writing about them and how they had done in the competition.

'Look, Dad! Do you think, one day, I might be in the newspaper?'

'Yeah, if you keep working hard, you might get in the *Plymouth Herald* one day,' he said, grinning.

'Wow, that would be so cool!'

The following year when I was 10, I went to the National Championships and was the youngest under-18 winner. The next day, a small article appeared in the *Herald* with the title: 'Diving Prodigy Daley is Youngest Ever UK Champion'. I was thrilled.

After that, the mentions in the local papers started to become more frequent as I had success at more competitions, and when I was 11, a TV crew started following me for a special episode on the BBC's *Horizon* series about Olympic hopefuls. As I went to my first Olympics in Beijing in 2008, the media attention ramped up and up, and soon I was becoming pretty used to having a microphone in my face.

After the Beijing Olympics, I became Britain's first individual world diving champion at ten metres when I was 15, and the press attention increased. I started doing feature interviews with all the major broadsheets and tabloids and I really enjoyed it. I loved talking about my sport, and there was never that much to talk about beyond that and school. Their coverage of me felt positive and supportive. Just a few weeks after a win in Rome in 2009 I was shot for Italian *Vogue* with Kate Moss by Bruce Weber. It felt surreal to be photographed by such a renowned photographer with a supermodel. I was lucky. I even asked Kate if I could take some pictures for my school photography project and she agreed, posing outside along a brick wall, whilst Bruce Weber gave me tips on how to take better pictures.

I participated in loads of amazing shoots and my media work was, and still is, a big part of my life. I had always enjoyed it and said yes to many interviews, sitting with journalists and answering their questions openly and honestly.

Before the 2012 London Olympics, I had always felt as though the press were on my side. Most of the coverage surrounding me had been positive or good enough, so I never felt the need to monitor what was being said about me. I was still a child and my profile was not so high. Reports tended to always talk about my sport, and sometimes about how I balanced diving with school work and family life.

But that's not to say that I don't have any questions around my portrayal in the media when I was younger. Sometimes I was asked to do shoots in my speedos and looking back they could potentially be seen as quite sexualised. At the time, I never said no to any suggestions by photographers about how certain pictures should look or what I should do. I just went with it. To me, being in my trunks was like being in my work outfit. The equivalent to a school uniform, or tie and jacket for an office job. I felt much older in my head than I really was, so I never felt like I was being taken advantage of. It did not feel weird or different; it made me feel grown up. I look back and think that would never happen now. I think people would have questions about how appropriate it was.

As I got older, though, the tabloid media really started to descend on me, trying to find out more details about my private life. The tide started to turn after the death of my dad. The paparazzi were all gathered unashamedly outside his funeral, waiting for me and my family to leave. There were loads of them in their jackets with long-lens cameras trying to catch pictures of us. They got their photographs of me, blindsided by grief, walking hollow-eyed behind his coffin, which were in all the papers the next day. Afterwards, in the run-up to London 2012, journalists would not stop probing about how I felt. Within a week of his death my private life was thrown open to all, and questions were being relentlessly asked at every turn:

'How does it feel to no longer have your dad around?'

'Were you there when he died?'

'How are you going to cope?'

'How do you feel?'

The agenda seemed to switch from support to getting something out of me: tears, an outburst, something new. Perhaps I wasn't as normal and well-adjusted as I seemed, but I certainly wasn't going to tell a random journalist how I felt when I couldn't even express the depth of my emotions to my family.

Then as my profile became bigger, it was like I was public property and everyone needed to know everything about my private life, where nothing was off limits. Once Lance and I got together, there were various stories about my relationship in the tabloids, many of which were taken wildly out of context. My relationship had become a matter of public interest. I'd seen situations where people had risen to the bait and tried to answer back to the tabloids and it never seemed to go well; I felt like it wouldn't matter what I did or said, so I chose to ignore it, despite the fact that everyone seemed to believe what they had read. The rumours and speculation around my private life felt very unfair. When lies are printed in black and white, or when the truth is twisted in a way to make it sound more sensational and that these stories will run, it can ruin a life in so many ways. Anyone who says, 'today's news is tomorrow's fish and chip paper' cannot have had their personal life under scrutiny, because after stuff is written, it's like you are forever tainted with it, however true or untrue it may be. I was also concerned that once stuff was written it would always be there, and my future children would read it. As a country, we have seen many people suffer at the hands of the tabloid media machine but still it rumbles on in the same way.

When stories about my private life started to appear more regularly in the tabloids, it made me feel so exposed and worried. I would feel nauseous when I saw my publicist's number flashing on my phone and would pick up, hesitantly, and dread hearing what they had to say. Even now, they text me first to tell me that everything is alright, so I don't panic.

It wasn't until around that time that I discovered certain newspapers were trying to trip me up. Often, my friends and

Lance's friends were called and asked questions about us, our lives and our relationship. There was a sense of 'digging for dirt', even if it was non-existent; it felt like they were scrambling around for anything to write.

One day my phone rang. It was my agent.

'I don't want to alarm you,' he said, nervously. 'We've had a newspaper on the phone. They say they have a video of you snorting a line of cocaine.'

'Hang on, what?'

'They say that in the video it is clearly you,' he said. 'And you are taking drugs.'

'Well, I have never done anything like that in my entire life. I'm an athlete and I'm drug tested all the time. Why would I decide to do a line of coke?'

Drug testers come randomly to test me at any time and demand a urine sample for analysis to show I don't use drugs. There are various organisational bodies involved in this process, including FINA and UK Anti-Doping, to ensure compliance. I fill out a form online stating where I am every hour of every day and where I sleep at night for every day of every week of every year. If they turn up to test me and I am not where I say I am going to be, I get a strike.

Three strikes and you are out.

It's serious: sometimes the testers turn up when I am at home, and at other times they come to the pool. I am probably tested once a month, sometimes slightly more frequently.

I've been doing this for many, many years and it's just part of the job. Even though I enjoyed going out for a few drinks with my friends, the idea that I could randomly have a Saturday night blow-out and decide to do drugs, seemed utterly insane and something I would never even consider.

'Well, they said they were going to run the story tomorrow and that if you want to comment, you need to comment by this evening,' my manager said.

'Well, I'm not sure – what I am supposed to say about something that I have never done in my whole life?'

I felt incredibly stressed. Lots of things had been printed about me that were not true but as soon as it is in the newspaper, everyone believes it. However, we were so confident that the story was not true, and that there was no video of me, that we did nothing. In the end, it turned out there was no video. Nothing happened or ran in the papers but I felt really rattled – it was the first instance where I'd really felt as though the press were willing to maliciously overthrow my career and reputation. I had seen in the past how my personal life was subject to twisting of the truth, but this was a whole new level.

That incident was the first time that I felt very out of control of the narrative that the media could paint of me. I know that I do not have the tabloids investigating my life on the scale of some other people, but it had still got to the point where I felt as if the newspapers were thinking of me as some kind of gossip fodder target. Everyone has an opinion about you, even if they have never met you. It seems you are judged by what is written. Now, I am never quick to judge anyone on what I read, however famous they are, and take most things in tabloids with a pinch of salt. Over time, I have learned to just accept whatever is written about me, even if it is not true, and move on. But sometimes it can feel hard to swallow. It is only if you refuse to allow stories to hurt you – and more than that, never define you – that you can truly become resilient to what people say about you.

Of course, as an athlete representing my country in a number of competitions, and a gay man who has what some may consider to be a fairly unconventional family life, it's not just the media's opinions that I have had to grow resilient to. I've always had a big following on my social media channels. I post the things I want other people to see and social media gives me the control to do that. I have an amazing following and huge amounts of support. At times, my platforms can feel like a community – a band of uplifting and friendly voices. However, it is not all positive and there are massive downsides. There are always voices in the midst of support, flinging homophobic comments or worse into the web. I do not see the vast majority of these, but occasionally trolls can cause real problems. After Pete Waterfield and I didn't get a medal in the synchro competition in 2012, I retweeted a message one troll sent me which read, 'You let your dad down I hope you know that.'

I had added, 'after giving it my all . . . you get idiots sending me this . . .' sending it to my millions of followers with an easy click. I have become more resilient to these kinds of messages, but back then I was still learning to not let it affect me.

After the guy in question attempted to backtrack, he then piled in on someone else who was defending me. He wrote, 'I'm going to find you and I'm going to drown you in the pool you cocky twat you're a nobody people like you make me sick.' It wasn't me at the receiving end of it this time, but it magnified the issue of cyberbullying. It is hurtful and no one should have to deal with it. I felt awful that I had been caught up in something so vile.

I have also been subjected to loads of homophobic abuse online. After the Olympics in 2016, a Christian group tweeted me telling me the way that I lived my personal life was why Rio had not gone well. Some days, I had it from all angles. Now I try to never read too much into the responses to my posts on social media, I post what I want to as I feel that is most repre-sentative of what I am doing at the time and hope that I never see the negative stuff, that it surrounds me like water in the pool and simply slips off me without me even really noticing.

The premise of social media and the way people can say negative things is bizarre. At times it can feel quite hollow, and it is always true that the one negative comment will stick much more than 100 positive ones. I have 2 million followers on Instagram, and so every time I post a picture I feel as though I'm standing on a stage and giving everyone the opportunity to shout whether they like what I am wearing/doing or not. Often in these scenarios, some people shout out stuff like, 'I hate your trousers', 'why the hell are you doing that?' or 'you will go to hell'. I know that most of the people who share negative comments like this on social media would never dare to say them to my face, and that they're likely only compensating for a lack of confidence in themselves. I've come to understand that social media almost acts as a barrier that people can hide behind when they are letting out their darkest thoughts.

Now, I tweet or I post on Instagram and I walk away. I think social media has given a platform for people to say awful things to someone else, and there be absolutely no recourse. I have learned not to care about what some faceless random or bot on the internet thinks. I hope that by the time Robbie grows up, the world has moved on and social media is just not a 'thing' the way it is now. Only by setting very firm boundaries around my social media use have I been able to use it positively and not allow the negative stuff to affect me too deeply. I try to use it to inspire me, and follow accounts that make me feel good. Everything else, I try to leave alone.

Over the years, I have learned to handle different pressures in different ways, some more successfully than others. I've learned to be very resilient in my sport and how to reframe failure and bad competitions, and to use positive self-talk. I have faced adversity many times and overcome it. Being the subject of unwanted media and social media attention is the area in which I have struggled the most to develop a resilient and tough mindset, but I have definitely got better at it over time and as my priorities have changed. Mean-spirited criticism, especially when it misinterprets who I am or my intentions, can be tough, but I do not have the energy to focus on it, so I try to rise above it. I never allow the opinions of others who are not close to me to get too deep. I seek out opinions from those I trust and respect, who will always give constructive advice. Do I sit around a table with these people, do they really know me and care about me, and therefore, do their opinions count? If they do, I listen. Otherwise, I try to just be neutral about it. I have taken that power back, and know that I can only control what is within my own power. When it comes to pressure from the outside, I know what I am doing and what is right for me and for my family.

KINDNESS

I remember the first national competition that I went to. I was 10 years old. It was the Senior National Championships and when we got the list of the contestants, there were eighteen of us on the list and many of them were a lot older than me. I felt sick to my stomach with nerves; everywhere I looked there were tall divers springing off the boards, twisting through the air effortlessly and landing gracefully without a splash in the pool.

'I'm so nervous. What if I do badly? What if I don't perform my dives as well as I do in training?'

Dad always had a way of making me feel better.

'Tom, there are eighteen divers in this competition. If you come last, you will be the eighteenth best in the whole country. How cool is that?'

'You're right. That's actually bloody brilliant.'

Instantly, all the pressure was off; it just slid away like water, evaporating in seconds, which probably contributed to me winning the under 18 national title and finishing third in the senior category for the whole of the UK that day. But I knew that regardless of whether I did well or badly, both my parents would treat me exactly the same. Even the most diabolical dives got a clap, a cheer, or even sometimes happy tears from my dad. Mum always said it was great like she believed it, regardless of how good the diving was. My parents were smart enough to know to not pressure or challenge me.

At quite a young age, I became my own worst critic if I was doing badly in training or if a competition did not go as it should. Once I had learned and executed a dive perfectly, I always wanted to recreate it in any competition. Sometimes I managed it but often, I made mistakes.

'That was awful, really rubbish,' I would mutter afterwards. 'I dived really badly.'

'Really, what do you think went wrong? I thought it looked great,' Dad would say.

I would then roll off a list of what I felt had not gone well.

From the start, I had the dogged determination and drive to win. A series of silver and gold trophies would sit glistening on the poolside and I wanted to add more and more of them to my special shelf at home. It was addictive and like a drug to me; the more I won, the more I wanted to win.

Some days, I hated learning new dives. I was scared. Often I would storm out of the pool and climb into my Dad's van, crying and muttering about how I couldn't do it and that the dive was too hard.

'You can go back into the pool and try it, or we can go and have a McFlurry at McDonald's. It's your choice,' he would tell me, shrugging his broad shoulders. 'I quite fancy an ice cream.'

More often than not, he would just be turning the key in the ignition and I would go back to the pool and have a go. We would drive home, buying an ice cream en route, and I would feel really proud of my achievement.

Every child wants to impress their parents and make them proud, but I knew I did not have to do well to earn any kind of love or respect.

It was always completely unconditional.

As a child, I saw other young divers around me who would go into competitions worrying about what their parents would think if they were not placed. They would glance anxiously, waving into the crowd, with a clear look of apprehension across their faces about what their parents thought and felt about their performance. I went into every day, competition or not, without that pressure. Mum and Dad both knew that when it came to diving and my school work, I just needed to feel safe when I was in my environment, whether it was in the pool, at school or at home, and then I could be my best.

There was never a time when they told me I needed to be 'something' or to do anything. Whether I won a competition or lost it, they treated me exactly the same.

I started diving because I loved it. I had the chance to dive and compete alongside people twice my age and there was no pressure. I had nothing to lose. I could just go out and have fun; I was simply having a good time. They saw diving as something I enjoyed, so they let me do it. They just wanted me to be happy and to never worry about what had gone before or anything that could happen in the future. Dad would say to me, 'Worry is a prayer for bad things to happen.' I guess he was trying to tell me to never focus on what I could not control, and if I thought about negative things too much, it was like I was willing them to happen.

Dad always had a great sense of perspective. He always pushed the fact that it was for fun and something I was meant to be enjoying. As diving started to get more serious, and on the occasions when the pressure of school work and diving weighed heavily on me, or I'd had a bad day for some reason, he would just say: 'Tomorrow is a new day, so you can choose to bring all that stress with you or leave it behind.'

I was pushed really hard by my coaches. As I progressed through the ranks, I went from just training in the pool to incorporating dry land sessions, where I did body conditioning and practised moves on the trampoline and developed my skills on the dry board, where you dive into a crash mat. The impact of diving into the water is huge, so this allowed me to practise my dives whilst reducing the stress on my body. I could isolate specific skills or parts of the dive and perfect them on their own before building up each dive. I would often wake up with aches and pains or be stretching after a session and would be agony, but my coaches and my parents would not show me too much sympathy or tell me I could give up. I was learning that this was just part and parcel of being an athlete. Andy instilled that sense of putting the work in to generate results. He would always say to me: 'There is no such thing as luck, just good preparation.'

As I got older and started winning more competitions, the pressure and expectation grew from my coaches and from within myself; the more competitions I won, the more I wanted to win. Learning to be kind to myself when I had bad training sessions or competitions took time. When one dive went badly, I would find myself falling into a downward spiral of negative thoughts.

'I can't do this dive.'

'This is a disaster.'

'I'm not a good diver.'

The whole training session would be completely written off, with me sitting by the poolside on the hard, cold tiles in tears. Any competition where the smallest thing went wrong would result in a disaster from that moment onwards. Some days, I felt I had lost even if I had barely started.

There was one local competition that sticks in my mind. I was about 9, and I was doing a front double somersault from one metre from the springboard. As I took my hurdle jumps to take off, my legs buckled beneath me as I took off and I landed awkwardly, slapping my back and my bum. I knew immediately that it would be a failed dive. I was mortified and so angry with myself, I ran away from the poolside and stormed out of the fire exit door, nearly knocking one of the other divers into the pool. One of the coaches had to come after me in an attempt to calm me down and persuade me to keep diving for the remainder of the competition. Even though I later placed fourth, that position was nowhere near good enough for me. Aiming high always comes with the very real risk of failure. All athletes are pushing the limits of what the human body can do, so it's inevitable that it is not always going to go well. Andy would try to coach me out of my negativity by using the Peter Pan analogy and telling me to 'fly out of it'. At the time, I thought that he didn't understand or 'get it', but as I grew up I was able to see that those analogies are good because they can help you develop a more resilient and compassionate mindset. I would walk away and stand under the shower for a minute or two and try to flip my thinking into a more positive, kind and encouraging mindset.

From the start of my professional career, Andy was trying to teach me to see each competition and each dive within that competition in isolation. You cannot focus on the outcome;

you can only focus on the process. Even when you have six dives in each event, and the first one may be a disaster, that should have no correlation to the next one. Or even if the first dive is great, there is no connection between that dive and your second dive. They are independent events and mentally I needed to see this.

I also learned early on that I could only control what I could control, never what was going on around me, so I needed to drop any expectation and pressure around external stuff. For example, in the same way that I have learned that I can't control what people think about me, I also cannot control how other people are performing. You can go into a competition thinking you can win and with everyone expecting you to win, but some days it's just a bad day, and it's someone else's turn to have a great day. I often feel this acutely at the British Championships where, as an Olympian, there is always an expectation from everyone – me, the coaches, the crowds, my team – that I will win. But when I start putting pressure on myself to win in this way, I can start to overthink it and ruminate on medals, and what it would mean if I didn't win one, which only increases my stress levels. Mindfulness has played a big part in what I do every day, and I now know that I need to be present in the moment and not worry about something that has happened or that is happening in the future. Many athletes will tell you that we spend hours and hours training our bodies and muscle memory, and fuelling ourselves with the right food, but if you can't train your mind and the way that you think, then you can never be your best. You can obsess over what has gone badly in the past or what might go wrong in the future but we only ever can control what is happening in that exact moment. In men's platform diving, where the degrees of difficulty are so hard, the points are high. I have learned that my inner voice is crucial in every performance and practising mindfulness, where I focus on my breath and being present in the moment, is so helpful.

There have been many times in big competitions where I have struggled to keep a positive mindset, but none more so than the Olympic Games in Rio in 2016.

There are so many fun, exciting, challenging things about going into the Olympics. Ever since I first asked my dad what they were, and he told me that the Games were the biggest sporting event on the planet and showed me the interlocking rings, I have had my eye on a gold medal. It lit a fire of enthusiasm deep in me and showed me that anything is possible, and if people work hard enough, they can compete in their sport alongside the world's best. It is one opportunity every four years to mentally and physically push yourself to deliver a once-in-a-lifetime performance, and to be the best, and I was determined to win. When I was just eight years old, I drew a picture of myself in a handstand, with a pair of Union Jack shorts on, and 'London 2012' with Olympic rings down the side.

So, the day they told me that I was going to be representing Great Britain in our own Olympic Games was incredible, and I have been lucky enough to be picked to represent the country four times.

Normally there are Olympic trials and various selection events to decide who will represent Team GB on the world stage in diving. The winner of the Olympic trial event automatically goes forward and the second place is at the discretion of Alexei, the Performance Director. He also chooses the synchro teams, and this is not always the same people. Whilst Pete and I were the two individual divers, and did synchro together in 2012, Dan Goodfellow who I dived with in Rio only competed in the synchro competition.

When it comes to Olympic selection, it is always hard as you're competing against the people you train with and see every day at the pool. In 2016, I trained alongside Georgia Ward who was expecting to go to Rio. She had come in the top eight at the World Cup, was a bronze medallist at the European Championships, and had done really well throughout the World Series events in 2015. Tonia Couch had already been pre-selected and there was an expectation all round that Georgia would make the additional place. When it came to the trials, Georgia was narrowly pushed out by Sarah Barrow, a diver I used to train with in Plymouth, and on the day, her ability to perform under pressure prevailed and she won the place. It can be very hard watching the disappointment and distress of your teammates, when they have worked so hard. It can be heartbreaking when you see someone put their heart and soul into something and it is taken away from them. It is mentally tough for everyone, and all you can do is be kind in the moment and try to offer some comforting words.

As athletes, we all work hard at not comparing ourselves with others, but at times we can be in direct competition with them; after all, diving is not a team sport and even synchro teams are put together on the basis of individual performance. When I compete at the National Championships, I am competing against my friends, so it can be a strange position to find yourself in. On the day after my dad's funeral in 2011, I went to the National Championships. I hadn't not won that competition for a long time, and on that day, Pete beat me and I came second. He could not let sympathy or anything else get in the way of the medal. The competition between us was a good thing and made us both strive to dive better. He was one of the best in the world and it was exciting to be challenging another top diver.

There are big diving centres in London, Plymouth, Sheffield, Leeds and Edinburgh, and divers are coming up through the ranks all the time. We meet at competitions and go on training camps and travel together. We cheer as loudly as we can for each other on the sidelines and afterwards. Despite this cama-raderie, the competitions themselves can be quite isolating experiences, and it is just you and your coach, trying to get the best score possible.

Balancing competition and friendship can be tough, but we understand that, ultimately, we are all competing to be the best in our sport. Everyone is always respectful of other people's feelings, and we are all hugely supportive of one another through the ups and the downs. I think many people can relate to the disappointment when competitions do not go your way, but other athletes understand the unique pressure and challenges that sport can throw at you.

After being selected for Team GB, you wait to hear about the 'kitting out' day, where we pick up all the different items we need. It starts with formal wear, where you are measured up for an official Team GB suit, then the opening and closing ceremony outfits, and then the athletes are moved into different sections to pick up all the different items and performance wear we need for our sport. There are literally thousands of different yet coordinated items of competition kits for all the sports. Mine was pretty minimal in comparison to some of the others, and included trunks, a towel and a pair of slip-on shower shoes. In 2008, I was too small for the men's 'XS' items, so my teammate Tonia's mum Sally made some adjustments, so everything fitted. Having swimming trunks that fit perfectly is really important because too much fabric can slow you down in the water or be uncomfortable. After the trunks didn't fit very well in 2008, I worked with Stella McCartney on the London 2012 version, and they fitted perfectly. She said it was the least material she had ever worked with, but no diver wants anything falling out when they are diving through the air!

In the run-up to Rio, the kitting out at Birmingham's NEC, and then launching the kit to the press alongside Stella and some of the other athletes, really brought home how close the competition was. The feeling of being one team and representing the country is an incredible one. This day just builds towards the excitement of the event.

The training prior to Rio was intense. When Dan and I had first started diving together, I never thought that we would have qualified for the Olympics for synchro because we had not been diving together for very long. We had been put together with an outside chance of qualifying the previous year. We had then won a bronze at the World Cup, and continued to win medals at every event we entered. My individual events in the World Series had also gone well, and in May 2016 I had won the European Championships in front of a home crowd in London with a total of 570.50, beating Russia's 2014 champion, Viktor Minibaev. I felt I was ready, physically and emotionally, to go to Rio and challenge the Chinese for a medal.

As a third-time Olympian, and aged 22, the expectations were sky high. I had gone to Beijing for the experience, into London with an outside chance of winning a medal, but

Rio was meant to be my peak because of my age, condition and the way I was performing. This was my chance to win a gold medal. I thought I was ready for it. I told the media that I would be satisfied with nothing less than gold. I was ready to win and then to step away from diving. I knew that I only had a certain amount of time left in the sport and wanted to go out on a high. I thought that Rio would be my time. My time to shine brightly and then to retire gracefully.

In the run-up to the event, nothing was left to chance. Our physical form was analysed closely. I was in great shape and felt good. We had some blood tests that looked at various levels, like iron, vitamin D and oxygenation. There was some evidence that we had been over-training, but I wanted to work hard and Jane dismissed this. We peed in a pot every day so our hydration levels could be monitored. Dan had relocated from Plymouth, where he had been training, to London. He lived with me for six weeks, and we bonded over *Games of Thrones* box sets and trained alongside each other every day. That was a big sacrifice, for Dan to move away from his home, but being able to work together rather than just seeing each other once a month or so for a training session made a big difference to our performances. I have had different relationships with my synchro partnerships over the years, but Dan is so laid back and it was very chilled at home, and professional when we were diving.

In many ways, being in the Olympic village at Rio 2016 there was less pressure than there had been in London because I was so cut off from everything. We had no idea what was going on in the outside world because there was less media around. The tempo felt calmer. All the athletes stayed in tower blocks like university student accommodation, and each country had their own one. The accommodation was actually pretty pared back and basic. Everyone assumes it is one big party but this was not the case for me, because my last event was one of the last two of the entire competition; so as everyone else was finishing, I knew I would have to maintain my focus. In Rio, the diving team had its our own apartment and we shared rooms with other athletes – I shared with Dan – and we got our heads down, training hard in the build-up to the competitions. In the run-up to our competitions we were given times to train in the pool and get used to being there in different weather conditions.

Like the other Olympic villages I had been in before in London and Beijing, there were spaces to unwind, such as a games rooms and a cinema room, and shops you would expect to see in any village, like a hair salon, and a post office so I could write and send postcards home to my friends. There was also a massive food hall about the size of three football pitches, where you could get any type of food that you wanted, twenty-four hours a day. There were also smaller dining areas dotted throughout the village. There was a medical centre, and a place for the GB athletes to go for physio. It was always good to see other athletes from other sports getting ready for their events. There was an amazing sense of camaraderie. We got around the village using Team GB Brompton bikes, which was fun.

Lance, my mum, brothers, and my Grandad Doug and Grandma Jenny all flew out to watch me. Friends and family were not allowed in the village and I could only see them at the Team GB lodge, which was a bus ride away, but I spoke with them and saw them as often as I could. It felt great that they were nearby and would be on the balcony.

The spectacular theatrics, lights and dancing of the Olympics opening ceremony is always such a ritual. I loved getting dressed up for the occasion – it made it feel so real. This time we all watched together outside the Team GB area on Union Jack deckchairs. Our first diving competitions were just a couple of days later, so it was decided that we would not march. I had previously marched with the team, and it always involved hours of waiting and standing, so could be extremely tiring in itself. Andy Murray was the GB flagbearer and we cheered particularly loudly as we watched him lead our athletes around the stadium.

My first competition was the synchro event, which was first included in the Olympics in 2000 and has been part of it ever since. In this event, we perform exactly the same dives simultaneously. The objective is to perform an excellent dive individually and also maintain the synchronisation between us. Like the individual competition, in each event we perform six dives with varying degrees of difficulty. The scoring depends on our execution and how in sync we are with each other.

In the synchro competition, nine judges score the dives. In the best synchro dives, we are exactly level, perpendicular to the water, breaking the water with a flick of the wrist at precisely the right moment. Four judges assess how we dive as individuals and five look at the synchronisation element of the dive, including how we mirror each other's movement, including the height, distance, rotation speed, and timing. The first two dives are compulsory dives with a limit of 2.0 degree of difficulty, to show control and synchronisation, and the last four do not have a limit on the degree of difficulty, so you can do the hardest dive possible as long as you are covering five groups within the list of dives. We leave the handstand dive out of the group as this is the hardest dive to synchronise.

Going into the synchro competition, we knew we had a chance because we had put in the work, but the competition was stiff. A few months previously, at the European Championships, we had been pipped to the post for the gold medal by less than a point in the final round, by the German pair Patrick Hausding and Sascha Klein, leaving us with silver. We did not want to let that happen again; I told Dan that we would get them back at the Olympics!

I was hungry for a synchro medal after Pete and I had finished in a frustrating fourth place in 2012. I always found myself extremely nervous at the start of the day, but once I had completed my warm-up dives and was more in my stride, I felt better. The pool was outside, and there was some confusion and speculation over the fact it had turned green, but the doctor told us that it was safe to dive in. In some ways it was useful because we could spot the blue of the sky and then the green of the pool. Before we knew it, spectators were starting to arrive and I saw my family in the crowds.

The build-up to any competition, and coming out to the cheers of the crowd, never loses its excitement and thrill. I love synchro because it allows you to work with someone else, and if you dive badly or dive well, you get to share that with someone else. Our names were announced and we waved at the crowd.

We had been given the start number of eight, which is randomly generated, so we were the last pair of divers and would have to dive after the Chinese. This was probably the most pressurised position to be in because we would be able to see our position in the standings immediately after each dive. Diving in an outdoor pool is a very different experience to diving indoors, and the weather can affect performance. I was nervous about the weather, but I felt we were ready for anything. We had trained in the wind, rain, darkness, and sometimes all three. We decided to just go out and do our best, and try to enjoy it and to be in the moment.

Our first dive was our inward one and a half somersault piked, which took us into joint third position and we stayed there for the next two dives: our reverse one a half somersaults, half a twist, and our inward three and a half somersaults. A slightly loose fourth round dive – reverse three and a half somersaults – saw us fall to fifth place but we moved back to third position again with our forwards four and a half somersaults in the fifth round. Going into the last round was our back three and a half somersaults piked. This was always a dive that could be our best but also our worst dive. I remember seeing Dan's face as we were standing on the board and he looked like a rabbit in the headlights. I felt exactly the same. There was an intense pressure – it wasn't like any normal competition: the pressure to win was multiplied by a million.

I remember standing at the back of the board and saying to Dan, 'Fuck it. We've got to give it everything. It's shit or bust.'

We kept our nerve. After landing we were not sure whether the dive had clinched the bronze, but after a second or two – although it felt like painful aeons longer – our position flashed up on the scoreboard. We had done it! We had won the bronze. We were overjoyed and leaped on each other on the poolside before falling into the pool for our seventh dive of the competition. It felt like such an amazing rush. The whole team rushed over to hug us.

The US pair, David Boudia and Steele Johnson, won silver,

whilst the Chinese duo, Lin Yue and Chen Aisen, claimed the gold medal. It felt so special to be able to stand on the podium together with Dan. All the thoughts that had whizzed through my head in London about winning a medal – I got to say all those things out loud to him because he was experiencing it too. I couldn't say it to my teammates because I did not want to be boastful, but in that moment Dan and I got to share our delight and talk about everything that had gone brilliantly that day. All those internalised thoughts came out in excited and joyful chatter. Later, after a long session with the media, we celebrated with our families, and took a lot of pictures with our new medals.

In 2008 and 2012, during the gap between the ten-metre synchro and individual competitions, we had moved out of the Olympic village to train at a different pool. In London, for example, I went to train in Southend between the competitions. We call it the 'escape strategy'. It allows us to clear our heads and not be caught up in the Olympic bubble with its highs and lows and corresponding drama. In Rio, however, there was no escape strategy because there were not enough pools within a suitable distance, so I stayed in the village and instead continued to train in the pool and watch all the diving competitions.

A couple of days after my synchro event, Jack Laugher and Chris Mears made history by becoming the first ever Olympic champions in diving for Great Britain when they won gold in the three-metre springboard synchro event. Watching them win that medal, I was over the moon for them. They had achieved my ultimate dream and goal in life: to be Olympic champions. It was an insane moment and the diving team just went crazy. We sang the National Anthem so loudly. I felt I had never been happier, yet so desperate for it myself in the individual competition at the same time. They had shown me that it could be done. I felt like I then had to do it as well. Then Jack went on to win an Olympic silver medal in the men's individual final three-metre springboard event. He had not had a good prelim competition or semi-finals but on the night, he went out and did it. In a strange way, it felt like there was more pressure on me to deliver. Waiting for my individual competition to come round seemed to take a long time. I was so, so desperate to make it my time.

Training every day in the run-up to my competition felt hard. The water was still green and felt cold. My sinuses had also started hurting and every time I hit the water, I felt like my head was going to explode. I went to see the Team GB doctor who gave me a nasal spray and antibiotics. After a couple of days I started to feel much better, but I never really knew until I was in the water exactly how I would feel.

One day I went down to the pool early to speak to the American diver, Greg Louganis, who is one of the best international athletes of all time, about everything that I was feeling. He was commentating on the event for the US. Greg is a four-time Olympian and won a silver medal in the 1976 Montreal Games, aged just 16. At the 1984 Los Angeles Games, he won the gold medal in both the three-metre spring-board and ten-metre platform events, making him the first Olympian in fifty-six years to achieve this incredible double. In the 1988 Olympics in Seoul, he hit his head on the end of the board during a reverse two and a half somersault dive from three metres in the prelims. Less than half an hour later, he got back up and executed the best-scored dive of the day, leading to a gold medal. He later went on to clinch the gold from ten metres, so he retained both his Olympic titles.

I was starting to feel the enormity of the pressure of the next few days, and he helped me to see it with a calmer sense of perspective and self-compassion.

'I would always offload all my worries and thoughts to my lucky bear,' he told me, reminding me of the lucky monkey I had as a child, that I took to every competition with me.

'Just take it all in, enjoy the experience, have fun and do your best. That's all you can do,' he advised. 'Treat the competition like it is just any other day with you and Jane, training together. No one else matters in that moment. You just have to give it your best shot.'

During the prelim competition, I found a sense of flow and my performance was almost flawless. After three dives I was in the top three; I felt great and was having fun. My forwards four and a half somersaults tuck, and reverse three and a half somersaults tuck scored 9.5s and 10s across the board. I knew I just needed a solid final dive, which was my backwards three and a half somersaults piked, and I scored 9s and 9.5s. I had done it! I finished with a total of 571.85, seven points ahead of Qiu Bo, my closest competitor, who had won the silver medal in 2012. My arms and legs were moving well and the atmosphere was incredible.

Heading home, everyone was asking for my picture – beating the Chinese in any diving competition is like winning an Olympic medal in itself.

I felt fired up for the real action and was ready for it. I went back to our apartment, had my ice bath and ate correctly. I was in bed early and slept much better than I thought I was going to. It felt like everything was aligned to go well. I started my day as I always did, by drinking lemon water and doing my Headspace meditation. I worked out that up until that point, I had completed 197 sessions and a total of thirty-two hours of meditation, and I hoped this could make a difference.

It was the last day of the competition, so there were a few changes on the poolside. Normally, Jane and I would go to the pool to train and warm-up before the event, and it would just be us there. On that day, there were the strength and conditioning coaches and managers from different teams all on the poolside with Jane watching me. I felt like it went really well, and was confident that out of the eighteen divers

I could make it to the twelve who would get through to the final, which was being held that evening.

I was also at the top of the leader board, so I would dive last. Being the last diver, following the Chinese divers, is a far better place to be than going first, although it adds a lot of pressure as you know exactly what you need to do and the scores you need to beat to make it through.

My first dive, the inwards three and a half somersaults tucked, was borderline. As I went back to the dry land area and put my eyephones in, my music wouldn't play – my phone brought up a message saying my account was frozen because I'd been out of the UK for a month. Being able to switch off and listen to music is an important part of my routine, allowing me to focus and relax between dives. So suddenly, I was sitting there in silence, finding it hard to not concentrate on what everyone else was doing. I did not think to have a back-up phone or music account.

I missed my second dive – my Firework – and scored just 47.25, sending me tumbling down the leader board. In a normal competition, Jane sits on the poolside watching. About ten divers before my dive, I usually go over to her and she gives me a few tips or pointers. For example, on my inward three and a half dive, she would tell me to stay tall, to do a big jump through with my chest in, to have wide arms for the entry and to take it nice and deep. She will just give me a few things to think about and a fist pump and send me on

185

my way. Then I go and do my dive and check in with her briefly afterwards and tell her I will see her in the next round. In the semi-finals, there is about half an hour in between each dive because there are so many divers.

Jane came over to the dry land where I was sitting and started pacing up and down. 'Are you OK? What is going on? Are you OK?' she kept asking, whilst pounding the dry land. I found it impossible to distract myself without music.

I knew if I scored highly in my remaining four dives, I would still be in with a chance, but on my third dive – my handstand – I scored my lowest score for a long time. I found this even more frustrating than the others, as this was a dive that has always been very consistent and steady; it was a dive that I never, ever dropped. I was flailing and I knew I needed to do something special, but I felt like I was on a downward spiral and I could not stop it.

There was nowhere to hide. I tried to focus hard on the next dive and move on to the next one strong and fighting.

There was something about that day. I stuck to my routines, but no matter what I did or what I tried to do, I could feel it falling away. I knew I needed to do something special. I could see that I was not the only one who was struggling. The Chinese diver, Chen Aisen, was putting in a flawless performance, but his teammate Qiu was also out of the qualification places at the midway point, although he clawed some points back with his fourth dive. David Boudia, who won the gold medal in 2012, was thirteenth going into the final round but later managed to make it to tenth place

My fifth dive dragged me up slightly, but by then it was too late. My body and mind were just not connecting, however hard I tried to force myself to do what I needed to. I needed 9s and 10s and over 100 points in total for a chance of making it with my final dive. I landed slightly short, scoring 50.40. I finished on a total of 403.25 points – 168.60 fewer than in the preliminary round. It was my lowest score in a very, very long time. I had literally gone from the top of the leader board and skidded to the bottom, in a matter of a few long seconds of diving.

It was the most heart-breaking moment of my entire diving career. I felt drained, empty and shocked. I almost couldn't comprehend how a few hours earlier I had dived so well, yet that day my performance had been abysmal. I could have done a hundred of my dives in training and maybe one of those hundred dives would've been as bad as every one of the six dives I performed that day. It was so easy to imagine how that day might've ended and what could have happened.

The level of emotion and heartbreak was the worst imaginable feeling; I had an awful tightness in my chest, like a hole had been punched into my heart. I had been building up to that moment my whole life, and I had blown it. It was so hard to comprehend and I had the same feeling of disbelief I felt when my dad died. On the dry land area, I couldn't stop crying and shaking. I knew I had to walk through the area where the media and the cameras were, with microphones about to be shoved in my face. I couldn't look the journalists in the eye and I could not speak without crying.

I knew I had to keep going, and said there and then that I would keep working towards Tokyo. The feeling of fire had come back, the urge to do better and be better was almost instant, but I felt devastated. My mindset had matured over the years and I knew I had to give myself the chance. Four years felt like the longest time to wait to do it again, but I knew that I had to try.

I know for Jane it was awful and she really struggled. Later she told me that when she came over to the dry land area during the competition, she had wanted to slap me to try to shake me out of my hole. I'm not sure if that would have helped, but I understood her frustration. I felt her disappointment acutely.

Afterwards, we attempted to analyse what went wrong. Jane wanted reasons so we could try to correct them; so the same thing could never happen again. There could have been countless reasons; maybe I had trained too hard, was exhausted and did not have the stamina to maintain the level of diving I had shown; maybe my music stopping and the changes in the routine had thrown me off; maybe, maybe, maybe, but honestly maybe it was just not my time. She kept trying to look for a reason and to blame something but sometimes there is no specific reason and you have to keep looking forwards. However we looked at it or dissected it, I knew I needed to be kind to myself and to not dwell on what had gone wrong, but instead look forward to the next competition. Blame is not helpful. I had tried to make the best of that competition, and I did not dive well enough on that day. I had to accept it. Many athletes go to the Olympics expecting to win and blow it. I wasn't alone in my misery.

My mum, after so many years of sitting on hard and clammy plastic seats and watching me perform from poolsides all over the world, told me it looked great and that she was proud of me. Lance said to me that it must have felt so shit, and it did; it felt utterly, utterly crap. We sat outside in the sunshine after the competition and I ordered myself a massive portion of chicken nuggets and chips. Lance told me that maybe it just wasn't my time and maybe our future child was meant to be sitting on the poolside when I won an Olympic gold medal. Maybe my story wasn't meant to end there. We were engaged and were thinking about our wedding and family, and I knew I had a lot to look forward to in the future. That helped me see the bigger picture and made me think about moving forwards. Everything up until that point had been focused on Rio. Now I needed to look beyond that. Everyone said the right things, but I was still heartbroken.

Of course, I watched the final from the poolside. I loved diving too much not to watch, but I felt completely numb.

Chen Aisen clinched the gold with 585.30 points. If I had scored the same points as I did in the prelim competition, I would have comfortably won the silver medal. But of course, you have to be in the competition to win it and I was firmly out of the running. As I started to process what had happened, a heaviness and hollowness settled around me like thick tar. It was as if I had to remind myself to breathe.

The closing ceremony was very wet and windy and we were all given ponchos for the parade. We walked in with all the other countries, and had shoes that lit up in red, white and blue that we needed to charge beforehand. There was Brazilian music and the crowds were going crazy. Despite the spectacle, I was just desperate to get home. I needed to take time off afterwards and just forget about diving for a few months. As we were clapped onto the plane at the airport by the airline staff, I breathed a long sigh of relief. It was over.

Dragging my suitcase through the door of our home, a few of my friends had come over to greet me. They had bought a load of eighteenth birthday balloons and hung them around the house because I had finished eighteenth in the individual event. It was like an eighteenth-place party. It was exactly what I needed and I laughed out loud. They showed me that they loved me whatever place I finished in. Some people might have been offended but it made me giggle. They have always shown me such kindness and in a funny way, wanted to celebrate what had gone right – the fact that I had come eighteenth in the world! Dad would've loved that. I remembered him sitting in his van: 'If you come last, you will be eighteenth in the whole country. How cool is that?'

We also celebrated my bronze medal in the synchro event and focused on the positives; I know Dad would've done this, too.

I did not drink for two years before Rio because I wanted to do everything right. Lance had also stuck to this with me in a show of solidarity and support. It was a perfectly sunny day and we went and drank prosecco and ate strawberries on the roof terrace, as the sun dipped below the horizon. I had a chance to decompress and chat about everything that had gone well and everything that hadn't. My closest friends and family were there and they understood. They have played a huge role in keeping me grounded over many years of diving and nothing changes with us, whatever is happening in my sport. We talked about the future: the wedding, our baby journey, our travel plans, and normal stuff. My friends' lives, their jobs, their relationships. I knew life would continue rolling after this, and the future was bright; I just needed to be kind to myself, take a step back, and to keep looking forwards.

I was desperate to just get away and have a proper break. I spent ten days in the UK and then flew out to LA where Lance was working on a show he had written and created called *When We Rise*. He was expecting me a couple of days afterwards and with a bit of covert organisation, I was able to surprise him at his production office. I spent a couple of months on holiday there doing normal things. We went out for dinner and hosted barbecues and I worked out. It was a great time to reflect and have some downtime. There were no post-Olympics blues this time. I think that only comes from doing really well. This time, I just needed some time to myself and to be kind to myself, before I returned, stronger than before.

I came back into the sport gradually. I knew I had to work harder to be better, and I worked as hard as I possibly could for a whole year. There was nothing that was going to stop me from being my best when I went into the World Championships in 2017. I began my training doing dry land work. Jane snapped her Achilles tendon and was unable to train with me, but fortunately my old coach, Peng, was able to move to London from Leeds, and I trained with him for a few months. He had a different style and our training felt quite laid-back. The year after the Olympics is always more relaxed and less hectic and I had nothing to prove that year. The training was less intense; I didn't need to keep pushing and pushing and doing the same dives over and over. Having the different perspective of being trained by someone else was helpful and I was determined not to hammer my body to death.

I tried to talk to myself in a positive and kind way; rather than saying 'don't do this' or 'don't do that', I reminded myself to focus on the process. Jump, swing your arms, come out of the dive quickly. I have seen and learned how detrimental negative self-talk can be, and that sometimes accepting a bad day for what it is does not define your life or your career and is the best way forward. You have to be kind to yourself, even on the worst days, and find the good points about it to take those forwards, rather than beating yourself up. Thinking negatively about the past only serves to feed painful memories and does not change it. I concentrated hard on taking the positives, however minute, from my sessions.

I focused hard on both training and keeping healthy, the small changes I could make to help me – sleeping properly, eating well, doing ice baths, being mindful, and those one per cents.

Going into the FINA World Championships in Budapest in 2017 felt like a huge event. It was with the same group of international divers I had competed against in 2016 in the Olympics, and I felt like I had a point to prove after bombing out at Rio. Having said all that, unlike in Rio, this time I had nothing to lose.

In the ten-metre synchro competition, Dan and I were pretty happy with how steady and consistent our dives were throughout the prelims, but one dropped dive in the final put us out of contention for a medal. Grace Reid and I also competed in the three-metre springboard mixed synchro event, where we won a silver medal. We were winging it slightly as we hadn't been able to train together that week, so we were delighted with the result.

In the ten-metre individual event, the favourite was the reigning Olympic champion, Chen Aisen. I imagine watching the final felt like a real cliff-hanger and we were fairly neck and neck, both of us scoring very highly for each dive across the board. Watching him put in perfect dive after perfect dive, I just thought: 'Watch this one. You do that, I'm going to do better.'

I felt my competitive drive ramp up and fan out to completely new levels – it was like I had blinkers on. After Chen had finished his final dive – a flawless Twister for 10s across the board – the Chinese team were going crazy and celebrating like they had already won, jumping out of their seats, whooping and waving their flags. They thought they had the gold firmly in the bag. I thought, 'OK, you want to play that game? I'll show you what I can do too.'

My final dive – my back three and a half somersaults – mattered. It felt like the dive of my life.

I remember launching myself from the platform and it was as if some kind of auto-pilot took over my body, I knew it was my time, I knew I was going to do it perfectly.

Ripping into the water it felt flawless and I had scored 10s, scoring a total of 590.95 points, just tipping Chen – who scored 585.25 – down the leader board. Standing on that top podium finally showed me, and everyone else, that I had clambered out of that deep Olympic hole and was firmly out fighting on the other side. It was a personal best score and a score that would have won the Olympics. It felt like redemption. By putting myself first and not focusing on external pressures, I had done it. My love for diving was back.

Over time, I have seen many good days and many bad days but, ultimately, every day is a new one. I knew then that if I was turning up, doing my best, learning more every day, then no one could ask any more from me. We are all imperfect, suffer and make mistakes. Sometimes when I have a bad day, I think about how I would talk to a friend if they made the same faults; I have got to a point where I don't want to turn any mistake into a bigger thing than it is. You can't waste energy thinking about what has been and gone in the past. For me, it was just unfortunate that I had a particularly bad day during an Olympic event in Rio. I have plenty of rubbish days in training but there are many, many great ones too. It's important to celebrate what has gone well. In Rio, for me that was winning a bronze synchro medal with Dan. I still came away from that event as a medal winner and I made a point of reminding myself, however sore I felt about the individual event. I always try to stay present in the moment as much as I can, and think about the here and now.

Self-compassion extends wider than the pool. I have learned that I need to be kind to myself and my body in many other ways. I need to ensure that I sleep enough, meditate regularly, spend time with my friends and family, disconnect from social media from time to time, take time to enjoy things that I love. This is integral to my happiness and therefore any sporting success. Every day, I write down three things I want to achieve that day; it might be a big one like performing one of my dives really well, it might be remembering to pick up some milk, or to pay a bill. It is not about striving to be more – it is about caring for yourself as you are. This, in turn, will always lead to greater resilience and happiness. It is also about looking forwards and never back. As Dad used to say to me as a child: 'Some days are good days and some days are not so good. It does not matter. Don't worry about it.'

PERSPECTIVE

Meeting Lance turned my world upside down. I always knew, almost as soon as we met, that I wanted to be with him forever. Every single part of him; the way he thinks, the way he acts, how he just is, makes me fall in love with him even more every day. Before we tied the knot, it just felt like a waste of time not being married. As soon as we met, there was a shift in my perspective towards being part of a couple and someone always having my back, whatever and wherever I was. I felt loved and safe.

We got engaged in 2015. I had bought a ring and had been hiding it, and was waiting for the perfect moment to ask the question – but so, it turns out, had he. It was just a matter of who was going to propose first. We were on holiday in

San Francisco and were in Dolores Park after dinner and I was building up to asking Lance to marry me. I had chosen this location because Lance had told me it was his 'favourite place on the planet'. I was slightly put off by lots of construction work going on around us, but it still looked picturesque; this was my moment. As I was about the get the ring out and drop to one knee, Lance started talking: 'This park used to be so beautiful and now it's really ugly with all this fencing.' The moment had passed.

A day or two later, we went to another famous park called Lands End. I was working myself up to it again. It was another beautiful day and we could see across to the Golden Gate Bridge and the shoreline in the distance. Just as I was fumbling around for the ring in my pocket, with one of our friends ready to capture the moment on camera, this large bunch of school kids came traipsing past chattering and laughing and I lost my nerve again.

On our return home to London, we went for a picnic in St James's Park one Sunday. Lance apparently had a whole speech planned and prepared that day; he was also ready to go. It was quite busy because it was one of those sunny London days, with friends and families out together. He waited for a quiet lull in the crowd and just as he launched into his speech, I noticed the next-door picnic blanket.

'Is that a nerf gun? Wow! Cool!' I obviously hadn't cottoned on to what was going on.

Later that day, we went out for dinner but we were practically sitting on the laps of the people next to us and there was no privacy at all. I suggested going for ice cream by Tower Bridge; as he stood up, I noticed a small box in his pocket and although I couldn't be completely sure it was a ring, I inwardly chuckled to myself, wondering who would get there first. As we approached Tower Bridge, there were press everywhere because there was a blood moon and they were all looking to capture a sublime picture. In the end, I was determined to ask him and proposed in the spare room of our house in my underwear getting ready for bed. Lance came out of the bathroom where he was getting ready and I was down on one knee.

'Wait there!' he said.

'What do you mean, wait?'

He dashed off to get his ring and then launched into the speech he had planned.

Safe to say, we both very much wanted to make it official. We were unsure how to announce it properly and ended up putting an announcement in *The Times*.

The announcement was in the births, marriages and deaths section and read: 'The engagement is announced between Tom, son of Robert and Debra Daley of Plymouth, and Lance, son of Jeff Bisch of Philadelphia and Anne Bisch of Lake Providence.'

We had put planning the wedding on hold until after Rio; as soon as the competition finished we started planning in full swing. We have friends and family all over the world, so it was hard to know where to hold it. We looked at loads of different venues around London but it was hard to find places that were big enough, or where there would be privacy. In the end, it was Mum who suggested that we look at Bovey Castle, which is set within its own private estate in Dartmoor, not that far from Plymouth. It is beautiful and as soon as we saw it and the area outside where they host wedding ceremonies, we knew that was where we wanted to tie the knot. In the end, we hired the whole of the venue and were able to invite all 120 guests to stay for the weekend. We set the date for 6 May 2017.

I loved organising our wedding. I got busy with spreadsheets and highlighter pens, organising the guestlist, table planning, colour schemes and the entertainment. Lance took on the business side of it all, negotiating with the various people involved. We loved it. I wanted a Union Jack – red, white and blue theme; in the end, we settled on burgundy, navy and white for our colour scheme. I met Burberry's Christopher Bailey when I was younger. We had bonded over the fact that he had also lost someone he loved deeply – his partner – to brain cancer. He made us special suits with our names monogrammed inside. Mine was burgundy with a navy tie and Lance's was navy with a burgundy tie.

On the day before our wedding, our wedding party and some guests arrived and we organised some entertainment in the grounds, like croquet and a birds of prey display. That evening we hosted a barbecue-style rehearsal dinner. It felt amazing to have all the most important people in our lives together, and some family members had not met, so that felt really special. My brothers were ushers, my cousin Sam was my best man and Sophie was my maid of honour, whilst Lance's best friend Ryan was his maid of honour and his brother, Todd, was his best man. My cousins, Malia and Brooke, were flower girls.

We stayed in separate rooms the night before the wedding and exchanged gifts in the morning. Lance bought me some personalised cufflinks and a Union Jack duffle bag. Tied around the bag's handles was a gift tag which said 'break in case of cold feet'. While I definitely didn't have cold feet, I was curious to see inside; breaking the tag revealed a bottle of vodka and a Diet Coke for my nerves. I had a special necklace custom-made for him, with a picture of our symbols for each other – a monkey and a frog – with our wedding date inscribed into it.

On the morning of the wedding we needed to make a decision about whether we held the ceremony inside or outside. The weather was overcast and in the end, we decided to stick with our plan and if it rained, we would get married in the rain. My mum insisted we started drinking early – the idea of having a glass of champagne with my breakfast seemed crazy, but I went with it. Just before we went down to the wedding, Mum, Sam, Sophie and I did a shot of vodka.

I walked down the aisle first with Malia, whilst the string quartet played 'How Long Will I Love You' by Ellie Goulding with everyone's eyes on me. It was so surreal and nerve-wracking. It felt very different to being on the end of the diving board at competitions. That aisle felt so long, like it stretched out before me for miles. You would think that I would be able to handle the attention but I am not great at being the centre of attention in that way. I couldn't quite believe it was my wedding day. I had never really envisaged how it would be, and seeing all the ladies' hats and flowers made me realise that this was it: I was tying the knot. I tried to soak it all in.

When I got to the end of the aisle I was relieved that I had made it without tripping over or doing anything stupid. Then catching sight of Lance as he walked down with Brooke, I was blown away. His hair was so golden and the blue of his suit made his eyes so bright. I couldn't believe that in the next half an hour he would be my husband. I felt like I had won the Lottery.

I couldn't help but feel really emotional and my eyes filled with tears. We had written our own vows and read them to each other. They described how we would value each other through hurdles and triumphs and be best friends, loving husbands and devoted fathers to our future family.

Lance said that when we kissed, the first thing he thought was 'vodka' because of how strong the taste was from my lips – we laugh about that now. As we signed the paperwork, the London Gay Men's Chorus did a flash mob and sang the Bruno Mars song 'Marry You' along the aisles. The weather held out and the umbrellas were packed away. We had everyone that we loved beside us; it was just idyllic.

We walked hand and hand into the reception to cheers and drank kir royales and chatted to our guests. Then we sat down for our wedding breakfast. We had designed the menu around our favourite meals we had eaten on our dates together. The starters were special chicken or veggie dishes, mains were bangers and mash, beef Wellington, or a veggie option, and puddings were cheesecake or sticky toffee pudding. Everyone gave speeches. We had a table of pictures of the people who could not be there. There were lots of mentions of my dad, and Lance's mum and brother, who couldn't be there, and the room went from laughter to tears as we remembered those who'd left us. The room was filled with love, joy and support for us.

The evening was such fun. We had a Union Jack Mini photobooth, where everyone had their pictures taken wearing silly wigs and outfits. I wanted to make my own cupcakes for everyone but in the end, I organised for the YouTuber Cupcake Jemma to make a multi-tiered red, white and blue cake for our guests. We also had a main cake and apparently it's an American tradition to have cake shoved in your face after cutting it, so I had a sticky face-full of icing and cake. There was dancing long into the night and by the end of it, most of the divers had their tops off and were flexing their muscles, and some of Lance's friends and family were wondering what on earth was going on. His aunts and cousins in particular, who are a bit older, were particularly enjoying it. It felt like such a melting pot of different people, traditions and cultures together in one place, just for us.

At the end of the evening we had fireworks set to two different songs that were important to us. As the colours cut through the black night and painted neon rainbows and patterns in the sky, I kissed my new husband. I felt truly happy and blessed. Lance is committed, sensitive, courageous, dedicated, hard-working, and he made me feel secure and like I could take on the world.

The next morning I was the most hungover I had been in all my life. I was sad it was over and that I had to say goodbye to so many people, but Lance and I were both as high as kites, despite our headaches. Being able to call him my husband and be part of that tradition felt momentous for both of us.

We decided to take a belated honeymoon as I was busy training towards the World Championships, which was just a couple of months afterwards. After we got home, we planted a Japanese maple tree on our balcony, taking time to pat the soil down, give it enough water and place it in just the right spot to grow. That was Lance's mum's favourite tree and we wanted to mark the occasion with her as part of it. We also painted our living room. How romantic?!

Then I was back at the pool training a couple of days later. I felt different after I was married. It changed my outlook and gave me an extra sense of security, and I knew how my life would then be. I felt safe, secure and supported.

Some days, I look back on our wedding video and remember all the special parts of our day. I can't wait to show it to Robbie when he is older, and go back to Bovey Castle and visit with him. The memories are priceless.

After the World Championships, we travelled to Barcelona, first going to the beach, seeing the sites and eating amazing food. After a couple of nights Sophie and her boyfriend Liam also came out to see us. Lance and I are both so busy working that we do not get that much opportunity to see our friends, so this seemed a great time to catch up with people. After that, we went to a golfing resort north of Barcelona for a few days, for some quiet time, just the two of us. From there, we flew to New York where we spent some time with friends, and then on to Hawaii, which was the main part of our honeymoon. This coincided with the Honolulu Film Festival, where Lance's TV show, *When We Rise*, was launched. We were really looked after and had an amazing time, seeing the sights. We flew over Hawaii on a helicopter tour, where we circled over Pearl Harbour, and saw all the picturesque water-falls and thick forests beneath us. We lazed around on the beach, broke some serious sweats on hikes, and went swimming with wild dolphins and turtles in the clear sea. It was bliss.

On our way home, we flew back via LA. I was lucky enough to be asked to sit for David Hockney. We had met and he had told me he wanted to draw me at some point. We had stayed in touch, and been to his house a couple of times for lunch. A few weeks before our wedding I got an email asking me when I was next going to be in LA, so he could complete the picture.

'Let's do this,' he wrote.

So, we went to his house and into his studio. As Lance tells the story, he knew it was going to take some time and did not want to interrupt the creative process, so he went away for a few hours – and he definitely remembers leaving me fully clothed.

'You know what, I haven't done a nude since the 1970s,' David told me exhaling a cloud of smoke and stubbing out a cigarette on the side of his easel. 'I think we should do a nude.'

'What? OK . . . !'

If there was anyone I would trust with this, it was him.

I started stripping off, thinking, 'Now what?'

'Sit down . . .' he said.

'Erm, how do you want me to sit?' I asked, trying not to giggle nervously.

'Just sit down. How you sit down, is how it's going to be.'

So I took my boxers off and hung them on the easel and sat, clutching myself as best I could, so as to not reveal too much. He started drawing and I just sat there naked as he worked.

When Lance returned the first thing he saw was my underwear hanging off the side of David's easel and me, just sitting there in his armchair, naked, whilst David focused hard on his work.

Lance laughed, walking over to David's picture. 'Is that an extra finger on his hand?'

'Those are his balls!' David cackled.

That picture, which is charcoal and crayon on canvas, is now hanging at the Los Angeles County Museum of Art.

Children had always been on the cards from day one for us as a couple. Coming to terms with my sexuality, one of the things that concerned me was the worry that I might not be able to have my own kids, or what the options were for same-sex parents. I've always been incredibly close with my own family, and I've always known that I have wanted to be a dad. Lance also grew up in a big southern Mormon family in Texas, so it was so never a question for him whether he would have children. We have always joked that we would only be happy if we had a football team of kids; we had both lost people very close to us, and wanted to build and grow our families again. In 2015, Lance and I started to research different options, including adoption and having children through surrogacy. Initially, I had no idea how surrogacy worked and I assumed it was one person having the baby and it would be their eggs used and that's just how it was. We did as much research as we could and we needed to decide if we went through the process in the States or the UK.

In the UK, surrogacy arrangements are not legally binding and laws do not protect the surrogate in the same way as they do in America. Though surrogacy is technically legal in the UK, unlike in some European countries, it is illegal to advertise that you are looking for a surrogate; the surrogate's name is automatically listed as the birth mother and her partner, if she is married, will go on the birth certificate as the father. There are steps to take to transfer the parenthood to the intended parents but it is not straightforward and a surrogate can change her mind about signing over her parental rights. There can be agreements made between the couple about this but it may not stand up in court. It is altruistic here, but there are downsides and the process is very complex and there are many things that can go wrong.

Lance knew people who had children via surrogacy in California. We wanted a child who was biologically connected to us; a baby who had links to my dad, Lance's mum, and those before them; genes that go backwards but can arch forwards into the future. This was important to us.

In the US, it is more regulated, and the surrogate is firmly in the driving seat. She chooses the intended parents and drafts the contract about how it will move forwards, and the parental order is completed whilst the surrogate is pregnant. We chose gestational surrogacy, where our surrogate would have no genetic relationship to the child, so an egg donor was chosen and then our sperm used to create an embryo that would be implanted into the surrogate who carried the baby for us. This is as opposed to traditional surrogacy, where the surrogate uses her own egg, so has a direct genetic relationship to the child.

In California, where we decided to go ahead, gestational surrogacy is legal, well-regulated and by far the most popular form of surrogacy. There are hundreds of steps that need to be taken in the correct order and everyone goes through rigorous screening and counselling to commit to the process, to make sure everyone in the 'team' is emotionally and medically healthy. Whilst it is legal and standard practice for a surrogate to be paid for the time she invests and the sacrifices she makes, this is never the main motivation, and due diligence is taken to ensure that any surrogate's driving incentive is to always want to help give someone a child who wouldn't be able to have one otherwise, over any financial gain. There are many generous and well-meaning women that want to be surrogates, but many do not qualify; in America this is not an easy process. It is not a given just because someone wants to be a surrogate. Nothing is left to chance. The fact that Lance is American also meant that, whether our surrogate was based in the UK or the USA, at least one of us would be doing this in a country that wasn't our home, so it made sense for us to choose the 'safest' option. We decided that this was what we wanted for our future family.

We went to have our first conversation at a clinic in Los Angeles in December 2015. They gave us a lot to think about but we both decided to freeze our sperm, there and then. We knew the process of finding an egg donor and then a surrogate might take years, but we knew that it was what we wanted, so we were willing to wait as long as it took and threw ourselves into the process. We kept our surrogacy journey very private, only telling those closest to us. This was something we talked about and agreed with our surrogate too.

Finding an egg donor is like finding a sperm donor. There are online databases with profiles of different women. Each one had a video of why they wanted to donate their eggs, along with some basic medical and health information. I know it sounds strange but it is a bit like dating; Lance and I looked through the countless profiles separately and decided who had the right attributes to potentially be a match for us and our future family. We agreed to make lists of who we liked, but in the end, I had only one name and so did he. The same profile had jumped out of the screen at both of us. We were struck by her in the same way; she seemed so happy and positive. We really never thought about what she looked like, we just wanted a happy and healthy child and someone who reflected us as a couple. She spoke about her outlook and why she wanted to donate her eggs, and the fact that she had seen someone in her family be unable to conceive and why she wanted to help other families have their own children. We felt overwhelmed thinking we had found the biological mother of our child. It felt like our family was complete.

Of course there are many legal, emotional and practical implications around surrogacy, and we used a special surrogacy agency who helped guide us through the process. The next step was to find a surrogate. Lance and I created a profile, talking about our lives, how we met, and who we are. We had to answer questions about each other. There is such a misconception in the wider world that surrogates are strangers to intended parents; this is just not true at all. The relationship was always going to be an incredibly close and intimate one for us, so finding someone who had the same interests, beliefs and outlook on life was important to us. Then it was just a matter of a potential surrogate seeing our profile and liking it enough to choose us.

When we got the call that someone wanted to meet us, we checked her profile and it was an immediate yes from us. Going to meet our surrogate for the first time felt like a monumental event. I was terrified; the stakes were so high. We really wanted her to like us and vice versa, as it would always be an incredibly personal journey. It took a few minutes for us all to relax but we had an instant connection. We had to be very candid and open. Over time, we built a relationship based on affection and trust. She was giving us this amazing gift and there was a warmth and kindness that was impossible not to fall in love with.

The eggs were fertilised, half using my sperm and half using Lance's, and then two embryos were implanted without knowing whose was whose. We did not want to know and it did not matter who would be genetically related. The child would be ours.

We walked through the clinical aspects of the process and how we would handle it and drew up a contract based on that. I remember seeing it for the first time and it was intricate and detailed, and rightly so; every eventuality of what could happen was covered and every possible scenario, so we knew what would happen. There was no 't' left uncrossed.

Once we knew the embryo transfer had taken place and there was a possibility she was pregnant, we were so excited, but at the same time we did not want to get ahead of ourselves because many things can go wrong in early pregnancy. Ten days after the embryo transfer, Lance went with our surrogate to the clinic to have some blood tests done. She already felt strongly that she was pregnant. It was a crazy feeling when we were told she was expecting our baby. Suddenly, it felt so real. We felt a bundle of emotions like many expectant parents: elation, apprehension, happiness, excitement. We wanted to make sure that our surrogate had everything she needed to keep our baby safe and healthy.

Despite the fact Lance and I were both travelling a lot for work, we were able to be there for quite a lot of the scans. It was magical to see our baby moving its arms and legs on screen. At our twenty-week scan, we saw that our surrogate was carrying a healthy, perfect little boy and we decided to share the news. I had learned that taking control of the narrative that gets portrayed about you is important, and this felt like one of the biggest occasions of our lives. We needed to announce it ourselves, somehow, before it got to the papers. It was Valentine's Day and we posted a picture of us holding a scan photo across our social media channels, saying: 'A very happy Valentine's Day from ours to yours', with an emoji of two dads and a baby. It was supposed to be one of the happiest moments of our lives.

Of course, we were inundated with congratulations, supportive words and warm wishes, but there was also a strong undercurrent of criticism, across both traditional media and social media, with a nasty spate of homophobic abuse thrown our way. The fact that we were two men having a baby seemed to be a problem for some. It felt like it was not just about our right to be parents, but also our use of a surrogate to have our baby that was coming under fire. There was a piece by a commentator in one right-wing newspaper in the UK about how it was 'not normal' to be two dads, with the comment 'pass the sick bag' and the fact that some women are used as 'breeding machines'. This brought with it a lot of debate and big consequences as many big advertisers withdrew their advertising money from the paper that supported this intolerant view. There was an outcry and people were upset, but many people still agreed with the commentator's sentiments. There was one radio show who asked their Twitter following if they felt there was anything 'sinister' about a woman carrying our child, and other sites drew thousands of comments by debating our choice and, ultimately, the existence of our future child. We would be lying if we said that these comments were not hurtful.

I understand there has been a long debate about surrogacy, and our announcement seemed to reignite the media's discussion around it, and provided a platform for people to argue it out, but who would want their unborn child to be part of that? Of course, we would never, as two men, be able to have a child without help from a woman, but there are incredible women out there who are willing to help heterosexual couples and gay couples have their own children, including the amazing surrogate that we had found. The vast majority of people using surrogates are straight couples who can't have children for different reasons, such as age and health. It felt like there would never have been the same drama if we were a heterosexual couple. There are many people in the public eye who have used surrogates, such as Kim Kardashian, Nicole Kidman, and Sarah Jessica Parker, and no one said anything. There was an element of concern about their health, and the feeling that it was amazing that there were women who would help another woman in this way. All of this negativity felt really challenging to accept because we wanted those first moments of Robbie being talked about to be happy.

The whole issue of wanting a family as two dads is a simple one. We desperately wanted to create our own family. Many people fall pregnant by accident but with same-sex parents, it is never an accident. It involves a different level of commitment and is always a motivated decision because those kids are always very, very wanted.

What does the modern family look like? There are so many different types of families. It must surely be rare to have a mother, father and 2.4 children, where everything goes perfectly and the parents stay in love. Ultimately, it is the people who devote their love, time and care to bringing up a child who are the best parents. This could be a single mum or a single dad, it could be that the grandparents are involved. Families come in all shapes and sizes.

We wanted Robbie to know exactly how he came into this world, so he could have all the facts at his fingertips when he wanted them. We started to write down every single step of what we had done and what was happening, so we would be able to answer every question he might have. There was never any question of our surrogate not being part of our family. From the start, we wanted her to be part of our future child's life growing up. Equally, she would never be our child's 'mother' because there was never a genetic relationship. But we are so close and speak all the time, we FaceTime, and we meet when we are in California. Our surrogate says she and Robbie are 'tummy buddies'. We have a profound love, admiration and respect for her, and we know she will always be in our lives and a member of our family.

As soon as we knew our surrogate was pregnant at the end of 2017, it suddenly felt very real. I was very excited but you hear so often of things going wrong in pregnancy that I was determined not to get ahead of myself. After all, I already had a whole drawer of baby clothes ready!

Every year at Christmas, I make Lance a small scrapbook filled with bits of paper and various mementoes of all the places we have been and experiences we have shared during our time together that year. In the first book I gave to him in 2013 after we met, I added a note saying, 'I will take you to Venice'. It obviously did not happen in 2014, or 2015, or 2016, so I think he must have forgotten about it! When I made the decision not to compete in the World Cup in 2018 because of my shins, I decided to finally take him away before Robbie arrived, so we could have a 'babymoon' – a last holiday where it was just the two of us. It also coincided with our first wedding anniversary, so doubled as the perfect anniversary getaway. I told him I was taking him for a date night and worked with his assistant to make sure his diary was clear for a few days, and I packed a secret bag for him. I said to be ready for 5 p.m. for our pre-dinner activity and we caught the train heading towards Brighton. Lance guessed we were on our way for a night by the sea. But instead, we got off at the stop for Gatwick and flew to Venice. We spent the most magical weekend in Venice, floating around on gondolas and visiting all the museums and galleries. It felt important to spend this time together before we became a family and were knee-deep in nappies and sleep deprivation.

We flew out to Los Angeles about a month before Robbie was due, and moved back into Lance's old house in West Hollywood. We hit the baby stores and walked up and down the aisles, making sure we had everything we needed to duplicate the items that we already had back at home in London, ready for our return. Picking up tiny nappies and wipes, and a car seat, made it become very real.

We knew then that our surrogate could give birth at any time, and that period of just waiting for the big day felt quite surreal. It was like we could never properly relax in the days that followed, and we would both be clinging tightly to our phones at all times, like some sort of life raft. We did not want to miss anything. As well as working out, I spent a lot of time reading and inhaling the information in as many baby books as I could. I like to be prepared. Before we left London we had completed a baby first aid course, where we learned what we needed to do if our baby choked or if they stopped breathing, which I think made us feel more confident. I was determined to be as prepared as I could be, but I found that the books completely contradicted themselves; for every book that said one thing, the next one told me something different. Does the baby need to sleep then eat or eat then sleep? Be left to cry? Or definitely not be left to cry? Fed on demand or fed on a schedule? I felt quite confused. Now when anyone asks me, the one piece of parenting advice that I would give would be: do not listen to any other parent's advice. I realised that once your baby is here, you just have to figure it out for yourself. You have to do the very best that you can and have faith that your baby will let you know if you are doing it wrong.

We played around with the different names we could call ourselves, and came to the conclusion that if our baby was still calling one of us 'Daddy' when he was 30 years old, that might be a bit strange. So, Lance became 'Daddy' which could change to 'Dad' when our baby was older, and I became 'Papa'. The new monikers felt special and would be unique to our new soon-to-be family of three.

In the end, the call came when I was in the garden, blissfully unaware and without my phone. One of our friends was cutting my hair. Our surrogate was overdue and had had no signs of labour, and was scheduled to be induced a few days later. In my head, that was when Robbie was going to be born.

Lance came running down the garden, saying, 'It's happening. We need to go!'

Despite the fact that we had been waiting for that moment for weeks and had everything ready, including our all-important 'go' bag by the door with everything we needed, I was still incredibly flustered, tripping over my own feet to get to the door. Our surrogate lives a couple of hours' drive from LA, and it was Friday afternoon, so we were really worried about making it through the rush-hour traffic. It was a pretty stressful drive.

Initially, our surrogate texted saying, 'I think it's happening,' and then what felt like minutes afterwards, our phones pinged again with the words, 'Yes, it's definitely happening.' It felt really surreal.

When we arrived at the hospital I expected there to be a crazy flurry of activity with doctors and nurses rushing around like they do in TV shows, wheeling hospital beds and shouting acronyms, but it was really calm and we sat with her, her husband and her best friend. Gay surrogacy arrangements in California are not unusual, and there is a huge amount of diversity there, so I think they were very used to it in the hospital. By this point, it was the evening and we thought that we would have a long night ahead of us.

In the end, our surrogate's labour was only three hours and about an hour after we arrived at the hospital, she was ready to push. We had known from the start that our son would be named after my dad, Robert, and have 'Ray' as a middle name. We used to call my dad Robbie Ray as he loved to sing karaoke, and we would all take the mick, calling him Robbie Ray Cyrus. Once I realised that Ray was a name in Lance's family, which also linked back to his southern Texan roots, it became the perfect choice for us. It was the name that we'd agreed together all the way back on our bike ride along the Camel Trail when we were first dating.

At 8.30 p.m. on 27 June 2018, Robbie Ray Black-Daley was born.

It was the most amazing and dreamlike experience; it's like I have the perfect words to describe the experience on the tip of my tongue and then I lose them again because they are not right. Once Lance had cut the umbilical cord and the baby had been weighed, I was the first one to have skin-to-skin contact on my chest. He was this tiny, warm squishy and long baby with the biggest, bright eyes that just locked onto mine, as if he was looking straight into my soul. Even though he was just a few minutes old, he was so knowing. It as an overwhelming and innate feeling of pure love. This was my little boy and I was his parent and there would be an invisible thread of love connecting my heart to his forever. The entire orbit of our universe had suddenly tilted, with Robbie now right in the middle.

Immediately he was rooting around, so we fed him and he fell asleep, his little face scrunched up and his eyes flickering. Our surrogate and her husband were both beaming from ear to ear; she was so happy and excited for us. She had given us the greatest gift and could never have given more of herself. There was nothing we could ever say or do to thank her enough. It was beyond words. There was just so much love and joy in the room. I knew that he would always be by far the best thing that had ever happened to me, more so than any career achievement or any other life moment. He was it.

We really wanted my mum to be there for Robbie's birth but we hadn't booked her a flight because she could only take two weeks away from work. At the time she was a financial administrator at a nursery, but also helped in the baby room. We didn't want to book too early in case she had to leave before the big moment, and it was hard to make a call on it. In the end, we got the call that our surrogate was in labour just as she was landing, and she got to the hospital with Lance's cousin, Debbie, half an hour before Robbie was born. All the other flights that day were cancelled, so it was as if it was meant to be; it was another part of our journey that was written in the stars. She got to meet him not long after he was born. I know that when I told her I was gay, one of her very first thoughts was about grandkids. She fell head over heels in love immediately.

We learned the most from the first twenty-four hours in the hospital, where the midwives taught us so much. As well as making sure Robbie stuck to the feeding schedule and that he had enough clean nappies, there were other skills we had to master like learning how to swaddle. That's not something you can practise without a live baby with flailing, teeny-tiny limbs. It was nerve-wracking, thrilling, scary, overwhelming all at the same time. Robbie passed all his tests with flying colours and we were discharged from the hospital the day after he was born. Before we left, our surrogate and her family came in to see us all and gave him a cuddle. It was a really precious moment.

The hugest moment of all was when we painstakingly strapped Robbie into the car, making sure everything was clipped and belted exactly as it should be – we had practised and done numerous dry runs – and shutting the door with a thud behind us. Suddenly, we were off, we were parents – Daddy and Papa – and completely responsible for the life of our son in the back seat. We were doing it.

The first few days at home were a steep learning curve, but pretty soon it was as if we had known him forever. My mum was with us, which was helpful when we went to look at him, stressing, 'He's asleep but is he breathing?'

She would reassure us, 'Yes, he's fine!'

For the first couple of days, Lance and I got up through the night to feed him every two to three hours, and change him together, and we would both sit up to make sure we were doing it right and passing the other one what they needed, like the teeny-tiny nappies. On the third night, we felt a little bit more confident to take it in turns and alternate so we could both get some sleep. Soon we spread out his feeds more, and I was doing the 10 p.m. and 6 a.m. feeds and Lance was going to bed early and doing the 6 p.m. and 2 a.m. feeds. I loved having a schedule and making everyone stick to it; that seemed to be my role in the early days, alongside cuddles, doing feeds and nappies. Robbie was just a great baby in every way; he was very chilled and slept and ate well. He was a million miles away from one of those screaming and red-faced babies that just seem angry. We joked that we had got a starter baby; the one they sent to nervous first-time dads. Like all new parents, we couldn't stop staring at him and thinking that every tiny thing he did was perfect. The perfect poop! The perfect coo! He was the most perfect – and most beautiful – baby on the planet.

We got into an easy routine. I would do my gyrotonics and work out, to try to keep my body sharp, and Lance would be typing away on his laptop whilst Robbie napped in the carrycot next to him, lulled to sleep by the methodical tapping on the keyboard, and joking that he was the perfect writing partner with no notes for him.

After four weeks, we flew back to the UK. The start of our journey did not go well and we arrived at the airport just half an hour before take off but, thankfully, after some pleading, they let us on. We were nervous about the flight but made sure we fed him on the take off and landing, and he slept the entire way. See? He really was perfect. We flew the first leg of the journey on a domestic flight to Dallas, because Lance's aunt Nan is an air hostess and she flies the Dallas to London route; we coordinated with her and she was working on our final leg home, which meant she could meet Robbie and talk to us as she went up and down the aisles.

We settled into life at home with the three of us. Robbie began to smile: a flicker of his gummy mouth open and his cheeks turning upwards. It was pure and unadulterated happiness, like a common human language, and we all just grinned all the time. As soon as he'd had his injections, we had friends and family around, so he was always being passed around from one person to the next and cuddled by different people, like a miniature pass the parcel, and he loved it. He was always happy. Early on my brothers came up from Plymouth to meet him, and all our friends came to be introduced. We were always keen for people to come and see the real thing, rather than just pictures of him.

Since then, some of our happiest family times have been when we are with our friends and family all together. We have always taken him out for meals, initially in his pram and later in a highchair at the head of the table, so he could get involved in the fun. He is a really outgoing and confident kid and we are so proud of him.

Going back into training after four months off felt different. And being a parent changed a lot of how I thought about my sport. My coaches had told me to take as much time as I needed, and I felt ready to head back to the pool. Becoming a dad had completely changed my perspective about the importance of diving. Now, with a child at home, there was no opportunity to obsess over work, and the good and bad dives I had done that day. I also knew I needed to make that time in the pool count; to train harder and work harder. I left my diving at the pool, and as soon as I was home, my focus was on what would happen with Robbie. It meant I could rest my mind away from my sport, in a way that I had not been able to do before. Everything in our lives now revolved around Robbie.

We found that as two dads, we could play to our respective strengths when it came to parenting roles, rather than being shoe-horned into those typical gender roles. I took over the routine and structure, and in the early days would jot everything down. It seemed to work for Robbie because he always slept and ate well. I love food, and so was keen to share this with him. When we started weaning, I happily did all the cooking and blending, decanting my creations into small portions to put in pots to freeze. It felt like a proper adventure. I found it so special to see him eat something, that I loved and just took for granted for the very first time, and the wide-eyed look on his face as he tasted the food. Broccoli! Sweet potato! Cheese! He would go through bowls of food, and soon I was giving him mini portions of meals and he grew so quickly. I cooked up a storm and have always given him curries, risottos and stews. He goes mad for vegetables and will always eat his broccoli before he touches anything else on his plate. Now he eats literally anything that I put in front of him. As he has got older he loves baking cakes and biscuits with me, stirring the mixture with his wooden spoon, and being in the kitchen together.

With Lance, he likes to help with the DIY and getting things out of the toolbox to help. Lance took a lot of the childcare on whilst I went to training every day. He sacrificed a whole year of his film work to be at home and I am grateful that he was able to take on that role and we were fortunate that he was able to do this. A super Dad!

After a year or so, we decided that as two working parents, the right thing for our family was for Robbie to go to nursery for a few days a week. It felt like a huge decision entrusting his care to other people, but during the settling in session he loved it so much, we couldn't get him to come home with us; he literally did not want to leave the other kids and new toys. He has always loved nursery and interaction with other kids. He is in his element when he is around other people, kicking a ball around in the park, or having a picnic. He always likes to help with stuff like watering the plants. We have become a bit plant obsessed at home and have loads of types, some in hanging baskets, some outside, and we even have a palm tree on our roof. Robbie has some of his own sunflowers, and plants in his room that he waters himself with his special watering can. He likes to feel grown up and he is very independent, so he makes his own breakfast – with help – and picks out what he wants to wear. He also loves being in the water and sometimes comments on the size of the splash, with an 'uh-oh'.

While I post pictures of our family life on social media, I am careful not to include Robbie's face. It is his choice whether he wants to be known in that way when he is older, but having a baby in the public eye can also come with a whole load of criticism and judgement. If I post pictures of us in the kitchen together, for example, and Robbie is sitting on the side, there are always comments by 'well-meaning' people about his safety, the fact he is eating sugar, or what I am doing right or wrong. Social media aside, as gay parents and gay dads, I sometimes feel like we are held to a higher level of judgment. When you are out in public, it feels like all eyes are on you to do the right thing or parent in the right way. It's not just on a practical level, like there often not being changing tables in the male toilets, for example, but I also think people see two dads and there is a feeling that we don't know what we are doing or that it won't come easily to us, in the way that it does to women. There are kindly offers of help, but at times, it can feel like we are doing a 'substandard' job, even if that is far from the reality. One day when I was on my own with Robbie on the train, a woman asked me if I wanted her to change Robbie for me. Another time, there was another stranger who tried to help me strap him into the buggy. He was about nine months old at that point, so I really had mastered it by then. I guess it is well-meaning, but can be unwanted, nonetheless.

I think when people see or hear about two gay dads, they are worried, but when they see us as parents and see that we love our son and just want to be a normal family, suddenly it all clicks into place and they realise that we are like any other parents. It can be hard being in the public eye as a gay parent, but it is only through personal stories that people can understand and be more accepting.

There have been other hurdles to navigate. Under UK law, Robbie's surrogate and her husband were still Robbie's parents, even though they were not biologically related. We had to go through two court hearings and show a lot of paperwork and documents to become his legal parents. It made me feel quite nervous, because before it happened, if he was in hospital having medical treatment, although we were clearly the parents any doctor could, in theory, decline our right to choose for Robbie, as UK law only allows a child's legal parents to make medical decisions on their behalf.

It was a challenging and expensive process to go through, to technically adopt our biological son. In the same month he said 'Dada' for the first time, we were called to court for a hearing to begin the process to legally become his parents – even though we were legally his parents in US. It was a good atmosphere, but then we were told that an inspector would come to our home to tell us if we were good parents for the child. It seemed incredible that someone would be sent to our homes in this way, so that they could judge us.

'It must seem very strange for you,' the judge said, seeing us both standing there looking nervous. She reassured us that it was both straight and gay couples who went through this particular inspection, but again it made us worry that we were not the same as other parents. It reminded us of the things people had said when we first announced our surrogacy. It made us feel uncomfortable and not 'good enough'; like we were an anomaly that the system couldn't deal with.

It involved a lot of time, expense and hoops to jump through, to navigate the process and make our son our own. It goes without saying that he has been worth every second, penny and leap, a million and more times over. He brings more joy to our lives than I knew was possible.

Lance and Robbie coming to watch me at competitions has always been problematic, due to the archaic rules around the sport. There was one occasion when he came with Lance to watch me at a London World Series event at the Aquatics Centre. It was a bit of a disaster because Lance had a run-in with British Swimming. We didn't want Robbie to be on camera, and we didn't want people taking his picture whilst he was sitting on Lance's lap, so we had made an agreement for Lance to have Robbie on the balcony in his pram. In the middle of the competition, a lady from British Swimming came over and told Lance off, saying it was not allowed, even though later that weekend there were other women with prams. Essentially, she was trying to kick him out of the venue, and we could not help but feel that had it been a mum and child watching their husband, they would not have been treated in the same way. It put Lance in an impossible situation – he wanted to come and watch me and support me, yet it felt like a targeted attack. He folded the pram away and left. I was then told there was an official complaint against Lance, saying he had spoken badly to the woman, but my grandparents had heard the whole encounter and everyone was completely baffled. There were no raised voices at all. The lady refused to back down, so in turn Lance felt that he could not come back the next day to watch me compete.

As an athlete, it can sometimes feel like you are 'owned' by your sport's governing body and they can treat you as they wish. I feel like I have done so much for the sport, but my family and I, by default, are not offered the same level of support as others. This is not the same across all diving nations. When we go to the World Series events in Canada, they have a space where family and friends can go and be together and generally get looked after. In the past, on the three or four occasions when I have competed in Canada, they have given Lance special accreditation to be in the area with the other family members.

Sometimes, it is as if we are still children coming up through the ranks. I understand that when I was a child I needed to be directed with calls of, 'Come on, kids' and told what time I needed to be in bed. Now, as a twenty-something-year-old man, married, and with a child, it feels less like I need that same level of direction. I know I need to get enough sleep to be able to dive well; I'm less keen on being told *when* 'lights out' is.

There are other ways the sport's authorities have been less than accepting of our relationship. There was a time back in 2014 when we were on the way back from the World Cup in Shanghai. British Swimming has these really random rules whereby athletes are not allowed to fly on the same plane as friends and family, or stay in the same hotel. I might understand separate rooms, but no, it has to be a completely different hotel, which can be difficult at times. Still, Lance dutifully stayed away in a separate hotel. On the way home from Shanghai, Lance was flying with Virgin and we were flying with Delta. When he had booked it, the times were five minutes apart. When we got to the airport, it looked like the flights were taking off at slightly different times but landing at the same time. It turned out the flights were a co-share, so it was the same flight that we would be travelling on together. At the time I didn't see it as such a big deal. My dad had always battled with this rule when I was a teenager. Often there were not that many flights coming out of a certain place, which would have meant having to stay an extra day, or leave early; it was never very easy for him. My family, including Lance, have always had to buy their own tickets, unless I am promoting the event for British Swimming. Some days, I just think it's easier to buy everyone tickets myself.

On this particular flight, there was a fire on our plane and we had to do an emergency landing. They were having to dump fuel, the air hostesses were crying and there were staff wearing hazmat suits; it was all pretty dramatic. We were circling a lake in Irkutsk, Russia, as they were trying to get clearance from this old Cold War airport to land there. Once we had landed, Lance had posted a video of it on his social channels, which drew some attention from the Virgin bosses. They were very helpful and moved us to the front of the plane to talk to us about everything that was being put in place to get us home. However, the team bosses continued to stick rigidly to the rules. We stayed in a hotel, and strangers were being paired up together as there were not enough rooms. There was an odd number of divers, so I suggested I shared with Lance. This went down very badly.

I couldn't help but think that things would be different if it was a heterosexual relationship and he was my wife. Even when we were married, we were never treated in the same way as straight couples. He is really tossed aside, and under-appreciated for the amount of support he gives me and my sport. I think this is true collectively of many families and the sacrifices they make. If athletes do not have their family and friends around them supporting them, then they can't compete. The bottom line is that I could not dive without the support of my husband, and now we have Robbie, without Lance's help, I could not train or go to competitions. He also has a career, and we are like most families, both working around our son. I think being a professional athlete and parent does not go well together, when the powers that be make it as hard as humanly possible. In our case, it feels even harder to mix work commitments and family life. The gender stereotypes of the mother being the one at home and the father 'working' are so firmly fixed in the sport psyche that it feels impossible to break away from that, and our family does not seem to fit into the mould, so it feels like they are not sure how we should be treated. In recent years, employers have been obliged to recognise that working mothers are able to raise children and do their jobs, and society as a whole has got better at accepting that dads – in heterosexual couples too – play a greater role in raising children than they used to. As such, the rules around parenting are changing in lots of walks of life. I feel that the world of sport has got a long way to go in that respect.

When I had Robbie I knew my life would never be the same again, but I never really appreciated how much it would change the way I thought about things. As well as training harder and being more focused when I am at the pool so I can devote my time and energy to Robbie when I am at home,

I am way more emotional than I ever used to be. I now see everyone as someone's child, so even when I'm watching a film or the news, I see things from a different point of view and feel everything more deeply. I cry more easily. My understanding, particularly for fellow parents, feels like it has grown exponentially. I have also found joy in some of the more simple things in life – tending to plants, cooking a great meal, walking around the park and looking at the flowers, having a picnic and doing lots of knitting and crochet.

Most of all, I feel that being a parent was always my true calling and my reason for being. Now when I go into competitions, I feel if I do well or I do badly, I can go home to my family who love me for me, and who will support me, whatever the result. It gives me extra confidence and allows me to take pressure away from myself. Of course I want to achieve great things, but being a parent and leaving behind some kind of lasting legacy, and passing on the lessons that my parents taught me, feels really special.

MOTIVATION

As an athlete, motivation is the foundation of everything I do; without the determination to keep going and succeed, everything else I throw at my sport – self-compassion, perseverance, endurance, focus, and so on – is meaningless. I honestly believe if you have the motivation to do it, you can achieve anything, and there will be nothing that can stop you.

As my career has unfolded, my motivation has ebbed and flowed to differing degrees. Just like anyone, I have good days and bad days – on some days it is simply easier to get out of bed and get on with the job than on other days. As my career has developed, I have learned to understand and accept this. On those days when I open my eyes and feel uninspired, weary or flat, and as if I am defeated before I have even started, I know I'll have to grind on and keep going – those are the days when I can make the biggest changes. I tell myself that getting up and going will always be worth it, and before long, something will click and my body will just leap into action. At the same time, I might adjust what I do in order to get the most out of that day, rather than push through and hurt myself. I might switch up some exercises, or alter my training schedule, so I will always make the most out of my time.

Since getting married and having Robbie, my family has been a massive motivating factor for me to work as hard as I possibly can. I want to set an example, work hard, and show Robbie that following your dreams is important. I want to make my family proud but at the same time, I don't feel the same pressure that I used to. Being a parent makes me want to work harder.

Going into 2020 – and another Olympic year – was exciting; somehow another four years had passed in a flurry of competitions and now I was in a different place, as a married man with a son at home. However, for me and many others, 2020 was one of the hardest years as far as my motivation was concerned. I couldn't wait to dive in the Tokyo Olympic Games, and then have time off to be with my family and take a break. My whole life revolved around four-year cycles of competitions and Olympics, and psychologically I was building towards Tokyo. The COVID-19 pandemic changed this narrative quite considerably, and added a whole additional year of intense Olympics training, which nobody could have foreseen. I imagine for all of us, it showed us that anything can change in an instant, that we need to live in the moment and focus on the positives in our lives. The end goal was still the same, and whilst the goalposts shifted I still needed to keep going towards the ultimate aim: to dive my best in Tokyo.

The first major setback of 2020 came when I broke my hand. It was the build-up to the National Championships at the start of the year, and towards the end of one week, I was in a training session and was tired after a heavy session in the gym. I was practising my front four and a half and I missed my hand grab, where I grab my hands around my legs. As I missed it, my hands smashed together. The dive was going fine at that point; it was just an accident. Seconds after climbing out the pool, my right hand was swollen and black and blue. I kept shaking it, willing the pain to stop. I think I probably have a pretty high pain threshold, but I could tell it wasn't going away.

After a few minutes, it became apparent that not only was it horribly painful and swollen, but I was struggling to move my fingers.

'I'll go up and do another one. It's fine,' I said, giving it a rub.

'You can't actually hold on to anything, so how are you going to hold on to your legs and do a dive?' Jane replied.

An X-ray showed one of my metacarpal bones – the one about two centimetres down from the knuckle of the index finger – was broken. At the start of any Olympic year, the last thing anyone wants to do is break a bone, though bones tend to heal quickly, without the need for surgery like a snapped tendon might. It was also my first broken bone due to diving, which seems pretty remarkable, thinking about it now. I knew that I then had no say over my training or what I could do. That's the frustrating thing about injuries; all control is stripped from you. I had to wait for it to heal. There was no other option. I knew that if I pushed myself I would just end up giving myself another injury, or it would take longer to heal.

I wasn't allowed to do anything for ten days, but I managed to work on other parts of my body in the gym. It was far from the ideal start to the year, and once again I felt those familiar ripples of frustration and annoyance. I was able to focus on exercises I would not do normally, such as strength work and cardio, stretching and rehab, and working all the little muscles I wouldn't normally have the chance to work.

The first time I actually did my front four and a half that whole year was at a World Series in Montreal, Canada, at the start of March, the day before the main competition. By then, the news surrounding the COVID-19 pandemic had been swirling for weeks and the Chinese were not at the event. We tried to continue as normal but like the rest of the world, outside of the competitions and training, we were hooked to the twenty-four-hour news cycle, with a sense of profound shock and lack of comprehension of what was happening.

By the time we arrived in Canada, my hand was near enough pain-free and I pushed to compete, again using the logic that if I was training my dives from ten metres, I should be able to compete them too. The event started well when Grace and I won a silver in the mixed three-metre synchro, behind the Canadian duo. During the individual ten-metre final, I was in the lead before a mistimed twisting dive meant I finished fifth. The UK teen diver, Noah Williams, who I train alongside, took the top spot. It was his first international medal and I was happy he won, but it reminded me how one wrong move or small injury can lose a competition. In hindsight, it may not have been the wisest idea to compete at all, but it is in my nature to want to dive at all costs. I knew that if I had not been injured, then that win would most likely have been mine, and that is incredibly exasperating.

We all wondered what Covid meant for our sport. At that point, the Chinese were not travelling, and it looked like Canada, France and Italy were not going to the next World Series event, which was due to be held in Kazan in Russia, a few weeks after the Canadian leg. We speculated about what would happen if the Olympic Games went ahead without divers from certain countries. I was torn; without the Chinese in the line-up, my chances of winning a medal would be far higher, but ultimately, I always want to compete in the fullest field. That's what I have always trained for. As we watched the world grind to a halt, and every other sporting event being shut down, it felt inevitable that the Olympics would be postponed or cancelled.

When we arrived back in the UK, Robbie had a bit of a cough and a sniffle, and at that point, everyone was being asked to self-isolate if anyone in their family had any of the three main covid symptoms. This led to another two weeks out of the pool. On 23 March, two days before I was able to go back to training, Boris Johnson made the announcement that the UK was going into lockdown. It was a moment of disbelief and I wondered how I would ever make it to the Olympic Games if I couldn't train. I had a bike and a treadmill at home, but not any weights or any of the other equipment I would need to continue training at the level that I was. The thought of staying out of the pool for weeks on end was unnerving. By that point, China appeared to be coming out of their lockdown. I had no idea what to think.

On 24 March, we heard the news that the Olympic Games were being postponed. I felt dazed and numb. There was talk and rumours on the elite athlete circuit of the event happening later in the year, in October 2020, or at the start of 2021; the hardest part was dealing with the unknown of what would happen, and when it would happen, if at all. Athletes like to control and to plan – it's in the job description. Obviously, waiting felt like a small sacrifice to make to keep people safe. Suddenly, the world felt like a pretty scary place.

Around five weeks into lockdown, we found out that the event was going to be postponed by a whole year. Psychologically, that was hard. I had August as the mental finish line in my head; a point I needed to get to so I could bow out on a high. I had planned to retire after the event. It felt like it was the right time for me. I knew my body would not handle another four years of training, and it felt like a natural conclusion. That was suddenly up in the air. I had tentatively started to map out my life post-Olympics, including where we would live and what jobs I might do, but now that seemed really uncertain too. So many questions rolled around my head: Can I do this? Do I really want to do this? Do I have it in me to work this hard for another year?

After a couple of days of mental wrangling, I decided that yes, I definitely wanted to continue. It would mean another year of diving, and that could only be a good thing.

Like everyone else, I was looking at the headlines every day and feeling shocked and saddened by the personal tragedies that were unfolding across every corner of the globe. Lance and I had been so careful to not catch Covid, and we didn't go outside for six weeks, staying in our flat and getting some fresh air from the balcony. We went out shopping for groceries, wearing gloves and masks, and were meticulous about wiping everything down once we brought it all in. We left nothing to chance. My mum looks after Robbie two days a week, and she was with us when Boris Johnson announced the lockdown. If she went back to Plymouth, we wondered whether she would be able to see us again, so we isolated in our flat together – Lance, Robbie, my mum and I. Lance continued writing, and I worked hard on my fitness in our lounge, and doing Zoom workouts. Having my mum there meant there was always someone to keep Robbie entertained, and we loved having her with us. The plus side was that I got to spend so much time with Robbie that I never would have had I been building towards an Olympic Games, which would have been jam-packed with training camps, competitions and preparations. I got to see him learn his colours, count to ten, and develop in other ways that I would never have seen if I wasn't around. The period out of the pool was also a good thing for me in lots of ways, and gave me a chance to rest my body and my mind. I did many different home workouts, ran on the treadmill, and did weights sessions to try to maintain my condition.

I also spent time practising my visualisation techniques, to help me envisage my diving routines. I use this every day that I am not in the pool anyway, and during this period it was particularly important. I visualise every part of the dive in my head, so it feels like I am never out of the pool. Doing this every day in lockdown took its significance to a whole new level, and helped me stay on the ball and motivated.

I also spent a lot of time knitting when Robbie was napping or in bed. I have never been able to sit and watch TV. I always feel like I need to be 'doing', whether it's the laundry, cooking or cleaning, and after a day training, I struggle to sit down and properly relax. Like any parent, there is always something in my head that I could be doing. I started knitting on the plane to that World Series event in Canada in 2020. Lance originally suggested that I learned to do it. He said lots of the cast and producers knit whilst they are waiting around on film sets, to take their mind off of their work during their downtime. I downloaded a YouTube video and tried to follow it on the plane. My first piece of knitting looked atrocious. I just couldn't get it. But whilst I was out in Montreal, on the poolside, I learned that one of the Russian springboard divers and one of the Australian springboard divers both knit and they helped me get started properly. They taught me the basics and my second effort looked much better. By the end of the trip, I had made a scarf. My obsession continued during lockdown and I started to set myself challenges like bright jumpers, hats and gifts for friends and their babies. It felt like a great way to be mindful. Knitting was another way to focus, keep calm and relax. It also forced me to physically recover and, literally, put my feet up. Later, I learned to crochet and now I flit between the two. It might sound ridiculous but I am so happy that I discovered it. It came at the perfect time for me.

The London Diving Team went back to training outside together at the end of June 2020, and then we returned to the pool in July. I was aware that if one of us at the diving club caught the virus, the chances were that we would all go down with it. I was also aware of the risks of long Covid. The stories I read about fatigue and breathlessness that lasted for months left me feeling daunted. Even the smallest factors can make the difference between winning and losing.

Now, as the 'dad' of the team, because I am the oldest and most experienced diver, I do feel like I need to set an example. However rubbish I am feeling, I have to put a smile on my face and get on with it. I want to bring out the best in others, as well as those around me. I want the other divers to see that however crappy I may be feeling, we all have it within our power to turn it around. If people are having a bad day, I can tell them that a bad session, a bad week, a bad month, a bad year, does not define who you are as a diver. I tell them that they need to keep going, keep diving, keep working hard and they will get there. I feel like I've had almost every diving eventuality thrown at me in the past.

We always try to keep diving and our training fun. I am always dancing and singing like an idiot or trying to turn our diving into a game to make it more competitive. We have a lot of banter; I try to point stuff out in a jokey way and encourage the other divers to do the same to me. If they give me a bit of trash-talk, I can give some back, and we sometimes wind each other up if we do a bad dive. Stuff like getting too close to the diving board, I'll joke that they almost took their own head off. I hope that it encourages everyone to do better. We also practise competitiveness in other things that I am rubbish at. We play pickleball a lot, as a warm-up, which is a bit like a mash-up between tennis, badminton and ping pong. This allows a greater sense of equality, and either enables me to rise to an occasion or practise losing. There are different winners every day, for different stuff that we do, and that makes it more fun.

Within our training, we try to turn as much as we can into a competition. For our line-ups, which can be quite boring, Jane will score us with a one if it is good, a zero if it is neutral, or a minus one if it's not good. We then add up our scores to compete against each other. I take spin classes for cardio, and put playlists together, and we have a great time whilst we are sweating. Or we even try to simulate competitions on training days, to try to put us in the best mindset possible. It keeps us on our toes.

The summer and second lockdown passed in a blur of training. Whilst the risk of Covid was ever-present, I was still enjoying training and having fun with the team. I knew we were lucky to be back at the pool when so many people's lives and work had shifted so fundamentally.

I had suffered another concussion during a training session on the day before New Year's Eve 2020, and I continued training for a few weeks afterwards. It wasn't dissimilar to my experience in Beijing. It was only when I missed my hands again that it knocked me sideways, and I was forced to take a week or so away from the pool. I wasn't training with the others and was up in the gym, separated from everyone. A few weeks later, it was a Monday morning and I started training but had a bit of a headache. I felt a bit dizzy still, but put it down to my concussion. I was talking to Gareth regularly about exactly how I felt.

The following day, my sore head continued so Gareth told me to take a lateral flow test so we could rule out Covid. It was negative, so we decided to take a step back from training. In theory my concussion had lasted a few weeks, so I went in for a brain MRI scan to check for any abnormalities. As my dad had brain cancer, there is always the fear that I could suffer in the same way as him. With any persistent injury we are normally scanned, but this one was clear and normal.

I continued to train with a bit of a dull, weird headache. On the Friday, I woke up with a really sore throat, like razorblades were in the back of my throat, but I continued as normal. When I went into training I took another lateral flow test, and again, it was negative. The sore throat disappeared after an hour or two, so I wondered whether I had just picked up a bug of some sort. I continued with my basic concussion training, which includes thirty minutes of cardio and some stretching away from my teammates, so I hadn't seen anyone that whole week. In the evening Gareth called to go through my concussion symptoms, as he had done every day, to see if they were getting better.

'I still don't feel right,' I told him. 'I know it's not Covid because I've taken two lateral flow tests, but I feel totally drained. I'm starting to get a weird cough.'

He told me to keep him up-to-date and I hung up.

After putting Robbie to bed, I quickly started to feel that something was very wrong. I had no chest pain, but all of a sudden I had a very high fever, and was either freezing cold or burning hot. My teeth chattered so hard and my skull ached. I hadn't felt that bad since I had pneumonia. Every time I stood up, I felt the room spinning and a blinding white light, as if I was going to faint, and as if I couldn't get enough oxygen into my body. Lance had to help me down the stairs and to the bathroom.

As I went to bed that night, I was nervous. I even checked that Lance would know what he needed to do if I stopped breathing. I honestly felt like I might die. With the lateral flow tests, and the knowledge that people in their twenties were often asymptomatic – they might just lose their sense of taste and smell, and didn't suffer badly from Covid – I felt like I must have a really bad chest infection. I necked as many painkillers as I was allowed, and resolved to try to see a doctor the next day.

After a fitful night's sleep, I woke up drenched in sweat and could barely do anything apart from lie on the sofa. I took another lateral flow test and it was negative again. As far as I knew, I hadn't been exposed to anyone who had Covid; like everyone else, my life was completely stripped back – I went to the pool and came home. I wore my mask and washed my hands religiously. I had not been anywhere else. My temperature was still high and I was breathless and unable to speak more than two words in a row. Getting up the stairs felt like an ordeal. I called 111 and they told me to take a PCR test. The nearest testing centre was a mile and a half away, and we didn't have a car. The thought of walking that far seemed impossible. I couldn't even say two words without coughing my guts up. I ordered a home kit to be sent to me, but I continued to deteriorate and the thought that it could be Covid suddenly seemed a very real possibility. By then my bones were aching all over and I had a hacking cough. My lungs felt pressurised, as if they had sacks of rice around them. I needed to get to that test centre and find out. I walked there very, very slowly, diligently avoiding everyone I could. When I returned home, I felt like I had been run over with a steamroller. Within eight hours, I received the message that I was positive.

Lance then started feeling sick. He was terrified of Covid, due to suffering with his lungs in the past. We were really worried about what would happen if we were both ill and couldn't look after Robbie. I started to feel better for a few days, but then my cough got worse again. My head felt like I had a vice tightening around it and my oxygen levels were dropping.

I called 111 and they sent a paramedic to check me out. They decided with my history of pneumonia, and some evidence that the new strains of the virus were causing chest infections off the back of the original infection, they took me in. Going into hospital in an ambulance with Covid was scary. I felt conflicting emotions: on the one hand, I felt bad because I knew the NHS, particularly in London where I lived, was so overwhelmed by the virus. I knew I was really sick, and it was Saturday night, so I wouldn't be able to speak with a normal doctor until Monday. I did not envisage myself dying, but I understood how quickly things could potentially go downhill. I had flashes of fear about whether I would be put on a ventilator, and my time being up. I was really terrified. They did blood tests and a chest X-ray. There were loads of blotches on my lungs. I was in hospital for about ten hours to monitor my sats, and they gave me some oxygen to boost the levels. Once they stabilised, they sent me home.

The days dragged past in a mist of aches and fever. It was like some sort of super-charged flu. Lance never felt as bad as I did, but there were days when he also felt very rough. Robbie showed no symptoms, and we did our best to entertain him, outsourcing some care to Disney+, which was a massive stretch for us, as we hadn't introduced screen-time to him before.

Three days after my trip to hospital, I started to make progress. As each day went by, I felt much better. The overwhelming feeling was a sense of relief that it was finally over. It had felt like a marathon of sorts, and mentally I wanted to very quickly put it behind me. It frustrated me how other young people were bending the rules to do what they wanted; surely I was an example of how catching the virus could be a bit like playing Russian roulette. I had no underlying health conditions and was at peak fitness when was taken ill. No one knows what hand they could be dealt. It was very humbling.

Once I had completed my isolation period and was completely symptom-free for a few days, I could go back to training. I was eager to return, but was reminded to not push myself too hard. I was put through a series of tests, and then I wore a heart-rate monitor during training, so I only ever reached a certain level of my maximum exertion. Just as in any part of my sport, there is a balance; when to push and when not to push. All I wanted to do was push, push, push, but I knew by doing that I would potentially push myself backwards.

The recovery period was a good chance to let me rest my mind and body, and relinquish control. I think that as human beings, and particularly sportspeople, there is a strong temptation to try to manage everything, and feel like we 'have to' be doing certain things. But ultimately not everything is always within our power to control. When things throw you off guard there is nothing you can do, and as soon as I had that positive test result, I knew I would have to go with it. Because it was Covid, it wasn't like any other virus, where I might have pushed myself back to the pool before I was totally ready to return.

My motivation remained high. With both my broken hand and Covid, I knew I had plenty of time to recover, and this would not scupper my chances at the Olympics. If it had happened at another time I would've panicked, and I think it would've been harder. I had to trust the process, to trust that I would be able to rehabilitate and that I would get back. I spent a lot of time doing visualisations to stay motivated.

When the UK went back into its third lockdown, the pool was closed to the public, but we were lucky that we were allowed to continue training there. We had to make some adjustments to our training schedule, but without that time in the pool, we knew we would have had to kiss the Olympics goodbye. The strangest thing of all was that the whole complex was in complete darkness, and they only ever turned the lights on for us. There was just one lifeguard that stayed the whole day, and the team, training in the different areas of the complex.

As athletes, we train for competitions, but with no events on the horizon there were periods when it felt like never-ending training. It was hard to summon the motivation to work as hard as we would have been if we were on the international competition circuit, especially with the knowledge that the Chinese elite team was competing with each other because they were in one bubble. It was a pretty sobering thought.

At that point, we were told the Olympics would definitely still happen in July and August 2021. It was finally confirmed in March 2021 that it would be going ahead, along with the fact there would be no overseas spectators. The fact that it was definitely going ahead felt like a relief, as I'm not sure I could have maintained the same level of motivation if it was postponed further. The idea of there being no overseas spectators was a bit disappointing, although it was not a huge shock as the international travel ban had been in place for some time. I had been looking forward to my family being with me, but I took the positives from the situation; in the past, I have always found it quite hard to meet with them, and it can be a bit of a logistical challenge. This way, at least I could solely focus on events.

We tried in the best ways we could to create the feeling of a real competition, and at the start of April 2021 we competed in a virtual event against Canada. It took some organisation, with the judges in different places around the world sending their scores in live, and a live stream to the audience, and it was strange competing without a crowd or any atmosphere. It was fun, though, and a bit different, and the team cheered as loudly as we could for one another, but it did not feel the same as a normal event by any stretch.

There was supposed to be a pre-Olympics competition in Japan in late April, which was eventually rescheduled for early May. It was hard to see how, with so many countries in lockdown, and only essential travel allowed in the UK at that stage, that they would ever get 240 athletes and fifty coaches on poolside, using the same gym and competing safely together in one space. We weren't told until a couple of weeks before the event that it was definitely taking place, and we were gearing up for it. After more than a year of diving with the same people, the anticipation of getting out of country and competing before the Games was at an all-time high. It felt like a bit of a blow when it was initially cancelled, but it was not a huge surprise to me – and when it was back on again, I still wondered whether we would get there. It affected my motivation in small ways, because everything still felt uncertain, and without firm dates it can be hard to stay focused. But I knew I had to be ready for anything in the run-up to the event. Not knowing what was going on felt like the overarching worry, and I knew that it was the people who would be able to handle that mental pressure, and keep working hard, who would do best at the event.

As we moved through the months of training, I felt good. My form came back. My diving was consistent. One of the main things I did during this period of having no competitions was visualising my dives, but not just that: I visualised competitions going well, and diving exactly how I would want to in any international event. I saw the judges, heard the noise, smelled the chlorine, touched my shammy. You have to feel everything and always mentally rehearse the perfect outcome. When there are 10s across the board, when I find my flow, when Jane is whooping and cheering from the sidelines. If you imagine things so carefully, I really do believe that you can make them happen – I like to think of my sub-conscious brain as a self-guided rocket that moves towards a programmed target. I think back to the picture that I drew of myself doing a handstand at London 2012 when I was 9 years old; the fact that I'd imagined winning gold for such a long time became my form of motivation to keep training hard so that I could make it happen.

If I visualise my dives in my head, knowing exactly how I could do my absolute best, that motivates me to get to the point where they are as good as I imagined. It is like giving myself the best mental warm-up. We all think in pictures, and even during lockdown and when I had Covid, and felt horrendous lying on my sofa, I still closed my eyes and imagined myself doing those dives. I knew I would be back at the pool at some point, and it gave me the drive and excitement to do it. It was like a mental videotape and if I didn't play it every day, I knew I would have a long way to go when I went back to training again. Winning just feels like a natural extension of imagining that win.

There were times after my concussion, and suffering from Covid, when I struggled with the sheer relentlessness of training, and the lack of travelling and the ebb and flow of a normal competition year. Some days felt so hard and challenging, and so often I felt like I just wanted to be with my family. But instead I kept doing my meditation, looking after myself, and stayed focused – I knew I was so close to the finish line. It was within touching distance. I had worked my whole life to get to that point and to fulfil my Olympic dream. I could not give up.

OPTIMISM

It's true that devoting hundreds of thousands of hours to honing technique and physical conditioning can lead to sporting success. But what I have learned over the years is that practice can only take me so far. The biggest key changes always involve my mental state – how determined, resilient, motivated and optimistic I am. I believe that the mind is the most powerful tool of all, and is what sets people apart when standing toe to toe with the best divers in the world. Everything else can be perfectly in place but if you are not thinking positively about the result, it's just not going to happen. If you think you can win, anything is possible.

As the summer of 2021 approached, the reality that I would soon be heading to another Olympic Games after a year's delay began to hit home. I was apprehensive about the prospect of going to the Olympics having not competed in well over a year, and so I was really excited to get some much-needed practice at the World Cup in Japan in May. I'd had to fight to dive in the competition, which was a qualifying event for the Olympic Games. I'd already secured my place and therefore the other two GB divers should have been there competing for the second spot instead of me, but I was nervous that the European Championships could be cancelled later that month, leaving me with no international competitions before the Games. I knew that if I was going to give myself any chance of diving well at the Olympics, I had to be there. It went to a diving panel to decide and eventually the vote fell just in my favour by three votes to two. After so many, 'will we, won't we?' moments and being stuck in London for fourteen months, finally being on the plane as it sped down the tarmac was an immense relief.

The Covid procedures put in place in Japan were extensive and very much enforced. At our hotel, all the food was brought to us in our rooms, and we were escorted from our rooms to go down in the lift with our country to train in the pool with only one or two other teams. When we were training, social distancing had to be observed on the boards, we had times for our dry land training that allowed for changeover cleaning, everyone wore masks and the seating was spread out. However, it felt like a small price to pay to be there and we quickly slotted into the new routine. Just to be in the very pool in which we were going to be competing in the Olympics in a few months' time was particularly significant. I felt very comfortable and at ease in the pool. Sometimes pools have huge windows with blinding sun glare, or giant screens showing your face that are always in your line of sight. In London, for example, there are enormous lights, and the curved shape of the undulating ceiling takes time to become familiar with. This pool had a similar structural set-up to London but there were fewer distractions; the screens were like basketball screens that faced outwards, so you could never see what they were showing, and the lights were unoffensive. I am hyper-vigilant, so for me this was a really good thing because it meant I could focus solely on diving rather than on my surroundings.

The World Cup was the first competition that I'd taken part in in recent years where there were no crowds; it reminded me of competing in the Nationals in the UK in 2005 and 2006 before my first Olympic Games, when no one used to come and watch me. The other competitors and their coaches were the only spectators, and when you came out of the water their reactions were a true reflection of how you had dived. There was no cheering if you performed badly, so if you heard whooping as you surfaced you knew you had done a great dive. It felt amazing. At this stage, I didn't know just how similar to these early competitions the crowds of the Tokyo 2020 Olympics were destined to be. Although I missed the buzz of the crowd, I felt grateful for the opportunity to be diving again.

I would be competing in the synchro competition with my partner, Matty Lee, who I had been paired with in late 2018. Matty was mainly an individual diver who was coming up through the ranks quickly. He had learned a new dive especially to be able to compete in the synchro with me; we had been put together in the hope that we would form a partnership that could qualify for the Tokyo Olympics. Matty had relocated from Leeds to train with me and the rest of the elite team in London. We got on with day-to-day training and were soon jokingly referring to each other as 'work husbands'.

Matty is someone who struggles with having lots of things going on in his head, and prior to this competition he didn't always manage to completely see the water during every dive. In this competition, though, he had a breakthrough. He nailed his 'spotting' and was becoming increasingly consistent. We found our flow and comfortably finished ahead of the Mexican and Canadian pairings. Throughout the individual event, I felt very calm and secured my second gold. There are details I want to address after every competition, but overall I was very happy with my performance.

Straight after the competition ended we were flown to Budapest for the European Championships. I was pretty exhausted and, after a year of spending almost all of my time at home, was really missing Lance and Robbie. We travelled for thirty hours straight to get there and only had a few days after arriving to recalibrate and fix our jetlag. It wasn't easy as I felt quite under par and started to get an ear infection, so I was put on antibiotics. It wasn't the ideal start.

In the synchro, Matty and I were up against the Russian A-team, Aleksandr Bondar and Viktor Minibaev, who had not been in Tokyo. Competing against them really pushed us and resulted in us scoring a personal best of 477.57. It was the first time I had won a gold at the Europeans and it felt great that we were seeing rewards from our hard work during lockdown.

In the individual event, I scored the highest single point score of my career – 109.15 for my front four and a half – but my tiredness got to me and I blew two of my dives. In my final dive, I could only score a maximum of 108 points, but Bondar, who was in the lead, was 108.15 points ahead of me. Even if I got '10s' across the board, I still couldn't quite catch him. I was determined to still complete the best final dive that I could muster, and the silver spot was mine in the end. Overall, I was happy with the result; I knew that all I needed was a bit of fine-tuning and sharpening up before the Olympics later that year, and saw these events as a valuable learning opportunity, especially after so long away from the competition circuit.

Despite having been excited to leave London, I was so happy to be returning home; it was the first time that Robbie had really been aware of me being away and I wanted to pick him up early from nursery, but they had planned a trip to the

London Eye so I had to hang on to see him for a few more hours. It was amazing seeing his face light up when he realised I was back and feeling his warm hands around my neck as he gave me a massive cuddle. He was grinning from ear to ear and so was I. Being away from him was hard, but knowing that any trips in the future would result in that kind of reunion was a comfort. In the few days off that I had afterwards, I was able to spend some time with my family.

Shortly after the European Championships, one of the coaches decided to run a mindfulness workshop and we all did some meditations. During the first lockdown in 2020 I'd torn some cartilage in my knee, but there was no pain and I continued to train. From then on, my knee would clunk and click all the time as I bent it, but it didn't give me any real trouble. After one particular meditation at this workshop, though, I stood up and my knee didn't click. 'Weird, I wonder whether it's fixed?' I thought.

As I began to move it got tighter and tighter, like a screw being turned. It became locked in a position and I couldn't straighten it or bend it. I wasn't in pain, but my knee was working in a much smaller range of motion.

The next morning, when I woke up, I could barely move.

'It's fine; I just need to warm up a bit more,' I said in my normal optimistic way, hoping that it would somehow loosen. I started doing some weights, thinking I could do the same exercises as everyone else but it was not happening.

'My knee doesn't feel right,' I told Gareth. I only ever say something like that to him when I think there may be something properly wrong.

Thankfully, Loughborough is a massive sports hub so there were doctors on site. We went up to see one, who examined me and we booked a scan. We thought maybe it just needed an injection to get it moving again. The doctor also mooted the idea that it might need keyhole surgery.

From there I was sent for an MRI scan. In your knee you have two bones and a piece of cartilage, called the meniscus, that sits between them and acts as a shock absorber; this is what I had torn in 2020. From the scan, we could see that the cartilage had not only torn, it had also flipped up and the joint had come back down on top of it. They call it a 'bucket handle' tear because part of the meniscus pulls away forming a handle-shaped segment of tissue, which was stopping my knee from straightening. It can be flattened and sewn back down, but the surgeon described it as being a bit like a bent credit card that may snap up again or cause more problems. The only other way to fix the problem was to take it out.

'There is a recovery time of four to six weeks,' the doctor said.

The Olympics were eight weeks away.

I knew I had to get on with it. As with all surgeries, there were risks and this one came with an increased chance of arthritis in that knee or numbness. They asked me several times if I wanted to go ahead because they knew the stakes were high, but being just a few weeks from an Olympic Games that I'd been working towards for five years and unable to bend my knee, I had no choice. With my knee permanently bent at a strange angle, I could barely even walk, let alone dive. There was no way I was going to the Olympics without this surgery. But despite the risks, I didn't feel hugely disturbed or distressed. I took a deep breath and agreed.

Rather than panicking, as I may have done facing this kind of surgery earlier on in my life, I looked at the positives: out of all the injuries to suffer in your knee that need surgery, having a torn meniscus is the best one. Apparently, it's a common injury for footballers and when they have the surgery, they can be back up and jogging on the pitch within a week or two. The recovery time was just within the window that I still had left before the Games – it would not be easy, but I was optimistic that I would be able to get through this setback.

I went to see the specialist Andy Williams at Fortius Clinic, who operated on Andy Murray's knee. I knew I was in skilled, safe hands. I wasn't given much time to dwell on my decision, as within thirty-six hours I was having keyhole surgery to remove the damaged portion of the meniscus. It took just twenty-five minutes. I had been struggling to sleep with my leg at a strange angle, so the overwhelming feeling when I opened my eyes after the surgery was one of relief that my knee was finally resting as it should.

I walked out of the operating theatre and felt no pain. I was determined to throw everything I could at my recovery and rehabilitation, and I knew I had all the right support around me. After a few days of rest, I started using different machines, like a flywheel and ice compression machine, to regain strength. I went to the pool and did a lot of upper body and core work. Obviously, it is never ideal to be injured, especially not this close to a major competition, but I started to look and think about what had happened as a good thing as it forced me to slow down. The temptation would have been to come back from Budapest and to hammer my body to the max to try to get the best result in Tokyo, but I'd gone into Rio having done this and felt so physically exhausted before the event. I had no choice this time but to rest.

Over the years, I have learned that, for me, the results of a competition never correlate with how many months beforehand I have been training. They are always about what goes on in my head. If my mind is in the right place, I will dive well and believe that I have every chance of winning. While I was recovering from this injury I wasn't able to dive, but I would still go up to the ten-metre board and visualise completing my dives, which felt as if I was actually doing the dive itself. I imagined launching into the air and disappearing beneath the water, scoring 10s across the board. I knew that optimism was a powerful predictor of how fast I would be

265

able to recover. I was not going to let anything stop me from smiling and moving forwards.

A couple of weeks after surgery, I was back in the pool, building my diving back up again. I started diving from ten metres and practising my individual dives and synchro list with Matty. Alexei came to watch our training one day, and I decided to complete my competition run-through for him for the first time since my operation.

'Tom, you are doing so well, that's it. Stop training now. You are ready,' he said.

'Um, but that's the first ones I've done,' I told him, grinning.

It showed me that doing all the things I could to recover – staying in shape, eating and sleeping well, doing visual-isations and remaining positive – really did work. I knew I had done everything I could to give myself the best chance of achieving everything I wanted at this competition – now I just needed to get there.

Around a month before leaving for Japan, we had days where we imitated the layout of our competitions, including simu-lating the prelims, semis and final of the individual event, and the timings and recovery between each stage of the competi-tion, which included massages, leg compressions and ice baths. It was a useful exercise to see how much time I had between the different elements of the competition and how it might feel, and to test out different meals and recovery sessions.

266

Some of my events were not great, but I started to look at these practice sessions as positive things, even when they didn't go as I'd planned. Of course, you want to do the best you can and for everything to be perfect, but if you don't make mistakes, how will you ever learn anything? We completed one practice run-through each week for four weeks in advance of leaving, so I knew I had the chance to improve for the next one.

'It's OK Papa, you can try again tomorrow,' Robbie told me one day, after a particularly bad day of diving.

Too right, little one. That's all I could do.

In the synchro events, Matty also had days that did not go so well, but I always felt that those bad run-throughs started to give us both the push that we needed when the training started to feel relentless.

We also started analysing our body composition more frequently; I was pretty happy with how I was going – I was floating at around 5 to 6 per cent body fat and felt light and ready. It was really important that my body felt the same and that my weight was consistent leading up to the competition, rather than me dropping a lot of weight just before. Even being a kilo lighter meant that I would move differently in the air.

A couple of weeks before we left, we transitioned from a heavy training period doing a lot of dry land work, including heavy weights and conditioning, into a 'peak' phase, where we eased off and did more aerobic and fast movement work.

The idea was that our bodies would then be completely primed and ready to go.

When it came to packing to leave for Tokyo, I felt a gnaw of apprehension. After five long years of training, suddenly the Games were right in front of me. The Olympics would soon be over and I couldn't quite believe that they were finally happening.

I hadn't unpacked my kit from the kitting-out day, so it was fun getting everything out again and deciding what to take with me. I also spent some time deciding which yarns to take. I wanted to knit something Olympics-related, and eventually settled on creating my own Team GB cardigan. I knew it would keep me busy and calm during the quieter periods of the Games.

It was finally announced that there would be no spectators due to a spike in Covid infections in Japan and that a state of emergency in Tokyo would run throughout the Games to try to combat the virus. Although it would be sad to not be able to feed off of the energy of the crowd, it would also have felt strange to suddenly be performing in front of thousands of people after so many months of diving in front of empty stands. The conditions would emulate how I'd been training, and the competitions up to that point, perfectly.

We were originally supposed to go to a training camp in South Korea before the event but it ended up taking place in London. Robbie went to stay with my mum because Lance was away working in Canada. It was hard saying goodbye to him but I knew he was going off on an adventure of his own. The plan was for Mum and Robbie to spend some time in Plymouth with my family and then fly out to Canada to be with Lance to watch my competitions.

After camp, we had a send-off at the Aquatics Centre before we were bundled onto the plane. It was quite nerve-wracking to hear that someone in the other diving squad, who trained separately from us, had contracted Covid. There was always a risk of being told to isolate or being pinged but we had to get on with our training and hope for the best. This positive result was a stark reminder that Covid was never far away, but I knew we were doing everything in our power to stay clear of it.

Once I'd packed everything and had arrived at the final training sessions in London prior to flying to Tokyo, I started to relax and focus fully on enjoying myself. Amongst other things, I waxed Matty's chest for him, which resulted in so many yelps and screams that Jack and Dan came in as they wondered what on earth was going on!

We were allowed to arrive in Tokyo five days before our event started, and we would need to leave within forty-eight hours of competing. I would be staying for almost the whole duration of the Games because the synchro competition was a few days after the start and my individual event was on the penultimate day.

Much like the previous Olympics, each country's athletes

were housed in different blocks, and with 376 athletes, Team GB and their coaches had a whole block. I shared our flat with the five other male divers competing for GB, and Matty and I shared a room. The flat had a balcony with an incredible view over the bay – we flipped a coin and got the best room. The village was also like those of previous Olympics except for the addition of millions of posters reminding us about Covid and the fact everyone was masked up. We had to wear plastic gloves to eat in the immense dining hall and every seat was separated with plastic dividers. We also had to spit in a pot every day to be tested for Covid.

We spent our time training on our own away from other countries, and it was exciting being back in the pool, which was all dressed up with Olympic rings. During my downtime, I FaceTimed Robbie as much as I could. I missed him but tried hard not to feel guilty for not being with him. I knew that if I was trying my best here, I was also doing the best that I could for him and our family.

My friends had sent me a gift to open when I'd arrived. It was a scrapbook filled with photos, messages, games, and even dares and a playlist they had made. They stuck in a label that had been taken from a vodka bottle they had waiting for me at home, knowing I hadn't had a drink for a long time. It was so special having personal gifts to remind me of home.

I also started knitting my Olympic cardigan. At first, I managed to knit the colours of the rings the wrong way round, so I had to unpick it and start again. At least it gave me something extra to do away from training. Knitting gave me something to focus on, but importantly, allowed my body to rest when I wasn't training. Whilst the other divers in the flat played computer games in the evenings, I just cruised in my own lane, knitting and crocheting.

After three days of training, which we had to do in isolation as we were from a high-risk country, we were put in a training group with the USA and China. It was good to be training alongside China because we hadn't seen them for ages. They were diving consistently but they weren't doing anything we were not expecting.

The day of the Opening Ceremony allowed us all to get dressed up together, and there was a speech to send the flag-bearers and athletes on their way. We dived that day and saw some of the rehearsals, where laser lights were going; the atmosphere was starting to build. We knew the mood would have been incredible if the crowds were allowed in but, again, I looked at the positives: life around the pool had been much quieter. For Matty, as a first-time Olympian, and many others, performing in front of a huge and noisy crowd can be quite overwhelming. Covid had made everyone's world that bit smaller than before and ours was no different.

The synchro competition was on the third day of the Games, so it wasn't long before Matty and I were preparing to compete. Unlike in an individual competition with preliminary and semi-final rounds before the final, in the synchro event, you go straight to the finals. Our chance of winning a synchro medal was literally down to just a few split seconds in the air.

As the synchro approached, there were times during the night when I was lying there, and my heart started racing as I imagined various outcomes. I channelled all the experience that I'd gathered on developing my mind over the past five years into visualising positive results. In the gym, I found myself hitting and surpassing all my power targets. It was mind-boggling that just a matter of weeks beforehand I had been in the operating theatre; I had a lot to thank my strength coach and the team around me for. I checked in with my family all the time and was happy to hear that Mum and Robbie had made it safely to Lance in Calgary. Talking to my husband and son helped me to feel positive and relaxed.

Watching the girls walk out for their three-metre synchro springboard event, I felt a huge wave of excitement, happiness and exhilaration wash over me. Unexpected tears started rolling down my face, as I comprehended how lucky we were to be there after the eighteen months that had passed. I knew I needed to enjoy myself and soak up every second.

I was so nervous watching the women's competition – I've always believed that it's much easier to be at the top of the board where you are in control of the next few seconds, rather than being a spectator, looking on. After every event there are both elated faces and distraught faces. The emotions ricocheted around the place and the energy was palpable. There were moments of sheer joy and elation but also of despair and utter disappointment. I had experienced all these emotions before but knew that life would roll around whatever had happened. I had made peace with myself and the pressure that I used to feel. I was as ready as I would ever be.

On the day of the synchro competition, I heard Matty rustling around through the night, trying his best to get to sleep. I think that we both had a pretty good sleep, all things considered. We did our saliva tests and headed to the dining hall, where we found ourselves having breakfast alongside the British gold medallist breaststroke swimmer, Adam Peaty. His competition was slightly earlier than ours that day.

'OK, let's go and get some golds,' he said grinning and standing up to leave. We had our game faces on.

It felt so surreal that the day had come but I was positive and calm; it sounds like a strange thing to say, but it felt like it was our day. We had imagined being successful at this event for as long as we had been diving together.

Warming up in the pool, Matty and I didn't have much to say to each other. We knew what we had to do and followed the plan. Jane had total faith in the fact we would deliver, and my relationship with her felt very different to how it had in Rio. We had worked through our disagreements and ups and downs and had got to a place where we understood each other, believed in each other and had found a sense of flow.

When it was time for the men's competition, we had to wait in the call room and Matty told me that regardless of the outcome, he felt that the previous three years we had trained together were the best three years of his life; he said I had taught him so much and he was grateful. It was a very special moment. I may have taught him a lot but he has also taught me so much. He is unhurried and methodical, whereas I move at 100 miles an hour. He is a creature of routine and has shown me the importance of patience and the merits of slowing down. He had taken his time to get into the swing of it in Tokyo and had found the first few days in the village stressful but had completely stepped up to the challenge.

We had to wait behind a big screen before we paraded out. Normally we would wait for just a couple of minutes but this was an eight-minute wait. It felt like the longest eight minutes of my life.

When our names were finally announced over the PA system and we walked out, we could hear the roar from the Team GB supporters and other people from around the world. It wasn't the same as it would've been with a full Olympic crowd, but it felt so special. There is a sense of camaraderie around the Olympics; you don't just cheer for your team or the people from your country who are competing, but everyone. Every athlete, every coach, every team member will have a unique understanding of the sheer amount of work involved in actually making it there and this always, always deserves a cheer.

Our start order was randomly selected, and it was decided that we would be diving fifth, ahead of both the Russian Olympic Committee and Chinese pairings. It was the perfect starting position for us to be able to put pressure on the two pairs that were considered our main competition. Our first dive was solid with clean entries into the water, and our second dive had probably the best synchronisation we had ever done. We ended up on 107.4 points, one of the highest scores we had achieved for our two required first dives. We were sitting in silver medal position at that stage, four points behind China, the reigning Olympic synchro champions.

I was cautious going into our third dive, our inwards three and a half somersaults with tuck, as I had been over-rotating in training, and in order to make sure I landed vertically I put the synchro a little bit out. On our fourth dive, our backwards three and a half somersaults with pike and a 3.6 degree of difficulty, we nailed it and scored a 10, which really started to pile the pressure on the Chinese duo, Cao Yuan and Chen Aisen. This is when they made mistakes and faltered and we moved into the gold medal position with a six-point lead. Round five was steady with 8.5s and 9s and we clung onto the lead, but the gap between us and the Chinese competitors was not very big. We knew we had to go big for our final dive – our front four and a half somersaults with tuck. I knew we could perform well and could handle the pressure and we dived like we would have had it just been Jane and the lifeguard in London watching us. It was a great one. We scored 101 points.

By that point, we knew we were guaranteed a silver medal because the Russian Olympic Committee duo, who were in bronze medal position, couldn't catch us. We quickly worked out that the Chinese, who were two points behind us, now needed 9.5, 9.5 and 10 to beat us. They had done it before and had received some generous marking that day. We knew it was going to be right down to the wire, whatever the outcome.

Standing with Jane and Matty on the poolside, time stretched; it felt like we were watching ourselves on videotape in slow-motion as the remaining pairs dived.

In their final dive, Chen and Cao disappeared beneath the water with barely a splash.

All we could hope for was that when their marks came up in the bottom right-hand corner of the scoreboard, it would say 'rank 2', making us 'rank 1'. The winners.

We looked. Waited. Looked. Waited.

It had been my dream forever, and I never truly allowed myself to believe it would happen.

Then it did. Boom.

The Chinese fell into rank 2.

We were Olympic champions.

All we could do was cheer and hug. Matty picked me up and then Jane came in for a group hug too. It felt like a riot of every happy emotion magnified by a thousand: joy, pride, exhilaration, delight, relief, satisfaction, redemption.

Then our teammates came running on to the poolside hugging and congratulating us; in the frenzy someone even managed to catch my chin and I started bleeding, but I didn't care. It was a whirr of cheers and joy and congratulations and disbelief.

I called Lance immediately and we both just kept saying I had done it. I was an Olympic champion.

Making my way to the podium, I realised I didn't have my wedding ring or Olympic ring with me, so I ran back, with the doping control team and Olympic organisers hot on my heels, so I could put them on.

Standing on the top of the podium, watching the GB flag go up and hearing the National Anthem play was truly incredible. I loved the fact that I got to share it with one of my best friends. As soon as the music started, I lost it and I couldn't stop the tears from streaming down my face. As I tried to sing, I couldn't catch my breath. The words stuck in my throat as the feeling of exhilaration and happiness flooded over me. The medal felt amazing around my neck. I thought about my dad and his giant flag. I wished he was there to see it. It was my moment on the podium but it was also for everyone around me and the team who had got me and Matty there. Lance is such a massive part of my success as well as my mum, family, friends, coaches and the whole of the diving team.

Afterwards, there was a whirlwind where everything was going on at once. There were photographers, film crews, and we had to take part in a press conference. There were cameras and microphones everywhere. My phone would not stop buzzing, ringing and beeping. It was insane. I tried to speak as coherently as possible about what our gold medal meant to me but it felt hard to put how I felt into words.

We were followed by the doping team and I went and filled out loads of forms and peed in a cup with them watching. When I got back to the village, it was the first time I could deviate from my normal meal of chicken, rice and vegetables. I tucked into a pizza and ice cream and it felt like such a treat.

I gave Matty a gold Olympic ring that I had brought with me from the UK. I was always going to give it to him, regardless of how we did on the day. My dad bought me mine after my first Olympics in 2008 because I was too young to get a tattoo and I wear it all the time, apart from when I am diving. Matty had talked about buying himself one and I had been encouraging him to hold off until afterwards. He was very sweet and said how much he loved the fact he would have a constant reminder of our partnership.

Lying in bed that night, I found it impossible to sleep and so at 11.30 p.m. I decided to go for an ice lolly. I thought back to all the times since I was a kid that I had dreamt of the day that I won gold at the Olympic Games. I thought back to 2018 when I couldn't even run down the board with my injuries and frequently gave myself concussions, and back to the aftermath of 2012 when I struggled so much with my Twister. I knew everything I had done to remedy that had worked. I also felt such an enormous sense of relief that I had finally done it. I had won many other titles but up until that point, I had almost felt like a fraud. I had been so lucky with sponsorships. Other athletes who had won Olympic golds did not have the same offers on the table. I felt the weight of expectation lift and I felt light in a way I hadn't for a long time.

I thought back to the time in 2020, during lockdown, when Lance, Robbie, my Mum and I were all together in our flat. We barely left but Lance and I would dedicate a night a week for a date night when we would cook for each other and come up with an activity. One of my ideas was painting canvases: we did three paintings and two are currently hanging up in our flat, but the third was so ugly it was never going to make it onto the wall. Robbie painted over it and on date night, Lance decided we would write on the picture what we wanted to achieve in the next five years. We then covered the whole canvas with gold leaf which obscured what we'd written, but seeing the canvas every day would remind us of our goals. Mine had words that started with 'OC': Olympic

Champion. In that day at the synchro competition, I had achieved every single thing I had dreamed of.

I woke up the following day, feeling a sense of peace. I packed my things, said goodbye to the team, and then went to the holding camp in Yokohama to get away from the high energy and emotion of the Olympic Village on our 'escape strategy'.

Jane was staying behind with some of the other divers because they were still competing but one of the other diving coaches, Alex Rochas, was there. I did a bit of diving and weight training and had physio whenever I needed it. I tried to use it as a time to rest and stay limber so I could hit the ground running again when I got back for the individual event. It gave me much more time to catch up with friends and family, and I spoke to Lance, Robbie and my mum as often as I could.

I spent the next few days training with Alex. The pool at Keio University where I trained only had a five-metre board, which they asked me to sign, so all the little kids could see it during their training sessions. That made me smile.

I started to feel really excited about the individual event. For the first time in my career, I felt content with everything I had achieved, so there was less pressure on me. I could then go out and dive as I did in my first Olympic Games. The pressure can feel like shackles around your ankles and can make you falter. I could see other athletes making mistakes; I felt for them immensely because I knew that feeling like the back of my hand, having experienced it in Rio myself. With our synchro medal, it felt like those chains had fallen away.

It was on my return to the village, where I was watching one of the competitions and knitting a jumper for a friend's dog on the poolside, that a picture of me and my knitting needles went viral. My knitting account on Instagram went insane. It felt quite surreal because I was just sitting there doing what I do every moment I can when I am not diving or with my family. I wasn't sure why people found it so interesting – because I am a guy, maybe? Whatever the reason, I found it funny. I never thought I would become a meme and be edited into different photos, but at the same time, I loved the fact that people might be thinking about taking knitting up as a hobby. I finished the GB cardigan that I started at the beginning of the Games and was very proud of it. I was happy to be flying the flag for 'Great Knittin'.

Most of my teammates had moved out whilst I was in Yokohama but it was great to be there to watch Jack Laugher win his bronze medal in the three-metre springboard event. It was a very emotional competition because there were a lot of divers doing the last dives of their careers and there were standing ovations around the poolside.

Going into both the prelims and the semi-finals for the individual event, my dives were not very consistent but, in both rounds, I did enough to get through to the next. In the prelims, in particular, it seemed crazy that I could dive so inconsistently and still come fourth, but we were all out of competition practice and these rounds were like a survival game for everyone. Any diver will know that both prelim and semi-final rounds are just competitions to get through and a job to get done, and even more so this year. Prelims are always hard because they are so long and draining and this event lasted three hours, so I was doing one dive every half an hour. I was lucky that I had my knitting because I did my dive then knitted for twenty minutes. That is what took me away from the competition. I was able to have those moments of calm before I started thinking about my next dive. I knitted a scarf for a toy that belonged to one of the camera crew. I needed to do something where I didn't need to count the stitches or think too hard about what I was knitting; it was just so I could be mindful.

I knew exactly how wrong the semi-finals could go after my experience in Rio. I had rehearsed that two-day period so much: what I was going to eat at what time; what time I would see Gareth for a massage; when I would have an ice bath; when I would do my leg compressions; which recovery supplements I was going to take and when. Compared to Rio, when we practised the timings but not extensively, we left no stone unturned. I needed to be as prepared as physically possible. I knew I had done everything I could in my prepa-ration but I still needed to go out and dive. No amount of preparation would bring with it the stripped-back nerves and adrenalin associated with an Olympic competition.

I FaceTimed Robbie before I went onto the poolside.

'I wear my Papa T-shirt for you, Papa. Papa do good diving!' he said smiling, with a little jump, and then spinning around, showing me his special yellow T-shirt which had 'Team Daley Tokyo 2020' printed on the front and his name on the back.

He was so sweet and it was a grounding moment. I knew he would love me, however well I did.

Standing out on the diving board, I knew I needed to not do anything stupid. I missed my hands on my first dive and it made my arms quite fatigued, so on my handstand dive, it was harder to keep the tension throughout my body. It was a slow start but as the dives ticked by, there wasn't anything that was going to stop me. The scores in comparison to previous Olympics were extremely low but I had made it through in fourth place again, behind Aleksandr Bondar and the two Chinese divers, Yang Jian and Cao Yuan.

I called Lance after the event and started crying with relief. It was such a different experience to Rio. I had overcome that hideous demon sitting on my shoulder and made it to the final. It was all upwards from where I had been five years beforehand.

The turnaround time between the semis and the finals was just a few hours. We'd practised moving between the events so much when we were back in the UK and I had found a way of using the time that worked for me; unlike some of the athletes who were rushing to get back to the village for lunch, I brought a cool box with me from home with ice packs and ziplock bags. I ate the same tuna sandwich and chicken sandwich that I always ate. I knew how much food to have and how I was going to feel. Having this plan in place made me feel more comfortable. I also did some leg compression recoveries and managed to speak to Lance again.

I knew the competition was going to be stiff in the final. I was in a good position after the semi-finals to put pressure on Bondar and the two Chinese divers and I was still at the business end of the competition, where the judges knew that we were the best qualifying divers. It was all falling into place.

Standing on the board to do my first dive, I looked down and thought: 'Wow. This is it. I'm diving at the Olympic Games. Not only that, it's my fourth Olympics and I already have three medals. I need to enjoy the hell out of this competition.'

I trusted in my training and preparation. Jane was the calmest I have ever known her to be. She could see that I had done everything in my power to get to that point and to get it right. I knew if I could remain positive, I would be able to achieve all I was capable of.

I scored 9.5s and 10s on my first dive and felt like I was putting my marker in the sand, and I leapfrogged to the top of the leader board with my second dive. In this competition, there was no time for knitting between dives. I was only sitting for two divers before warming up and getting ready.

I concentrated on breathing, so my heart rate never went too high.

It was on my fourth dive – my handstand – that I started to feel the strain of the previous missed dives in the earlier rounds, and I used as much adrenalin as I could to keep pushing on; I dropped a few points, but my overall score remained high. I always knew that a breakaway group would form at the top of the leader board with me, the Chinese divers and Bondar, so I expected there would be contention for the medals. As it happened the gap between me, Cao, Yang and Bondar widened. I was aware of where I was and it brought comfort to be near the top but I knew that one missed dive could cost me my medal. I needed to fight to try to catch the Chinese divers.

Going into my last dive, my back three and a half somersault piked, I poured every last ounce of energy and concentration into my final leap. As I climbed from the water, I felt a sense of immense pride and happiness. I hugged Jane, and took a deep breath. I had won a bronze medal and my fourth Olympic medal. Watching Cao and Yang dive after me and secure their medals, with Cao making history by becoming the first Olympic diver to win golds in three different diving events, was phenomenal. They are pretty unstoppable force and the scores were huge. But regardless of what anyone else had done, I knew that if that was the last dive I ever did, then I would be happy and proud of everything I had achieved.

*　　*　　*

Standing on the podium to receive my medal I reflected on how I have put my whole life into diving, and how so many people around me have devoted themselves to helping me win those Olympic medals. It is almost incomprehensible for me to think about the number of people who have had an impact on my life, career, and journey as an Olympian. Everyone from my family and coaches to the barista at my local coffee shop or the people who come over and say hello when I am doing my grocery shopping. It's like a jigsaw with me in the centre and hundreds of pieces of different sizes slotting carefully into position around me, holding me together. I am so grateful for my army of supporters.

The medal hung solidly around my neck, but despite feeling the weight of the metal pulling down, the heaviness started to fall away from my shoulders.

The immediate aftermath was a blur of interviews, cameras, microphones and drug testing. Noah Williams (who had also competed in the individual event) and I were the only GB divers left in Tokyo. Mark England, Team GB's chef de mission, put a bottle of champagne in our flat and we went to the coaches' room to pop the cork and do a toast with Jane, Gareth and some of the others. We then went to hang out with some of the other divers for a night of celebrations. I didn't know when I was going to see them again. I was so bone tired I initially considered going to bed but knew I would look back in many years and wonder why I did not enjoy the fact I had just won two medals in one Games. I decided to worry about feeling crap in the morning. We had a fantastic time, and I watched the sun rise and then had to pack my bag to go home. Initially, there had been plans for me to stay for the Closing Ceremony, but they were keen to get the athletes home quickly. I found myself sitting in my economy seat the following day when one of the cabin crew came over.

'Your boarding pass has been printed wrong,' he told me with a wink. 21A had been scrubbed out and replaced with 1A. I had been upgraded. I climbed into the seat and passed out.

All my friends were waiting for me at Heathrow and had organised a minivan that was decked out with Union Jacks and bubbles to bring me home. They had rented a house to watch the competitions in, so they could stay up all night and be together, and had ended up having a sleepless and boozy weekend, so I think they were pretty glad I was feeling tired and hungover. We had a bit of a party on the way back, but after getting in we ordered an Indian takeaway and took ourselves off to bed. I still had a lot to look forward to: I couldn't wait to meet my new niece Myla, my brother Will's little girl, and a week or so later, I would be reunited with Lance and Robbie.

What are my plans for the future? I will be taking a year out. There is a new event coming to the Paris Olympics – the mixed synchro, which I really enjoy competing in – which is something to think about, but I am in no hurry to make any decisions. I have always wanted to go out on a high. I never wanted to be one of the athletes who say they have retired, only to return to the sport a year and a half later because they have missed it too much. Over the next year, I know I will be able to see my life a lot more clearly. Having finally achieved the medals I've been striving for all of my life, I will be able to map out the future and maybe create some new goals, and I will be taking everything that I've learned about myself with me. But family will always be my number one.

When I told Robbie I had won another Olympic medal, he said: 'Papa, when you come to see me?'

And really, that just put everything into perspective. Love wins.

ACKNOWLEDGEMENTS

Huge thanks to:

Georgina Rodgers, for capturing my voice and, quite frankly, being some form of therapist for me!

To Lisa Milton and the whole team at HQ, for being all-round brilliant publishers to work with. To my fantastic editors, Zoe Berville and Abigail Le Marquand-Brown, and to Georgina Green, Harriet Williams, Kelly Webster, Rebecca Fortuin, Joe Thomas, Dawn Burnett, Kate Oakley and Halema Begum.

To the YMU team: Alex McGuire, Holly Bott and Amanda Harris, for your unwavering support at every step.

To Megan Carver and Jacob Beecham at Carver PR, for their formidable PR expertise and help.

ACKNOWLEDGEMENTS

To Jane, for seeing me through my last years of diving. To Andy, for starting me off with the help of Peng. And, of course, a huge thank you to my synchro partner in crime, Matty. We achieved our dream together!

To Mum and my family, for helping to make my dreams possible. I am so grateful to you.

To Sophie, Liam, Joe, Leah, Tom and Simon; the best friendship group I could ask for! Thank you for being so understanding of athlete life.

To Dad, for everything you did for me. I will never, ever stop loving, remembering and celebrating you.

To Lance and Robbie, for everything. You inspire me every day, you are the reason I carried on diving. You are my reason for everything. I love you.

ONE PLACE. MANY STORIES

Bold, innovative and
empowering publishing.

FOLLOW US ON:

@HQStories